Harold F. Weitsz

21-day *Spiritual* Transformation

basileia
PUBLISHING

Transforming our Lives
Changing our Circumstances
Appropriating God's Blessing

21-day *Spiritual*
Transformation

Harold F. Weitsz

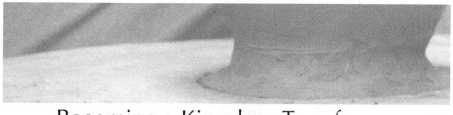

Becoming a Kingdom Transformer

The Great Transformer

Isaiah 64:8-9 [NLT]

And yet, O Lord, You are our Father.
We are the clay, and You are the potter.
We all are formed by Your hand.
Don't be so angry with us, Lord.
Please don't remember our sins forever.
Look at us, we pray,
and see that we are all Your people.

The Potter skilfully and competently shapes each vessel, TRANSFORMING it into the design of His choice.

Allow the Master to transform you into a vessel of honour and glory, fit for His use and well pleasing to Him.

First Published in South Africa by Basileia Publishing 2009
c/o Hendrik Potgieter and Falls Road, Little Falls, South Africa, 1724
HAROLDWEITSZ.COM | www.haroldweitsz.com

Author: Harold F. Weitsz
Editor | Production Editor: Maud Weitsz
Copy Editors: Linda Vermeulen, Louis Begemann,
Adrian Wright and Charmaine Gaffley
Technical Editor, Cover Design and Layout: Charmaine Gaffley
To report errors, please send a note to charmaineg@littlefalls.co.za

ISBN 9-781920-333119

A Special Thank You

I give praise and glory to the Father for His immeasurable grace and undeserved favour that He has so abundantly poured out upon my life and the lives of those He has entrusted me with. The words of King David are an echo of my heart and I praise the Lord for the opportunity of writing this book

Psalm 62:5-8 [NLT] Let all that I am wait quietly before God, for my hope is in Him. He alone is my rock and my salvation, my fortress where I will not be shaken. My victory and honour come from God alone. He is my refuge, a rock where no enemy can reach me. Oh my people, trust in Him at all times. Pour out your heart to Him, for God is our refuge.

I firstly dedicate this book to the Congregation of Little Falls Christians Centre who for over two decades have faithfully supported my wife and I on our Kingdom-of-God journey. I salute you for your loyalty and consistent devotion to the Lord and His church of which we've had the privilege of shepherding all these years.

Secondly I want to thank my wife Maud for the hours of work that she has spent in capturing my notes and thoughts so accurately. Without her work and the faithful editing team that assisted her, the quality of this book would have been lacking.

Lastly a special thank you to my daughter Charmaine who came up with the very appropriate cover design, depicting the Father as the Great Potter moulding us into vessels fit for the King.

A Personal Note
From the Author

It has been my privilege to have encouraged thousands of believers annually to join me on the 21-day Daniel's fast. I have seen this discipline transform and change many lives through the years. Believers have been inspired and encouraged to make the transition from nominal Christianity (in name only) to becoming true and genuine Christ-followers, radiating and living the life of Christ on a daily basis. Too often we rely on other people to help and counsel us when the solution lies in a personal relationship with the Father through a powerful interactive prayer life. Jesus told His followers that although He had to leave them, He would send a Helper, the Holy Spirit, to stand by and help them overcome the evils that would befall them in this world.

We hear the word 'transformation' being bandied around by politicians and world rulers in their plight to win voters' hearts. In spite of good intentions and well intended ambitions, **only a 'transformed' person can bring about true and lasting transformation.** Through six thousand years since Adam, man has tried to change and transform this chaotic, confused world with his own ideals and standards, but the result has led to increased chaos, disorder and confusion. I would venture so far as to say that it is the Tower of Babel all over again as man aspires to become like God, enforcing his rule and ungodly moral values on society.

Only One True Government

There is only one true government, the government of the Kingdom of God. There is only one 'Transformer' and His name is Jesus. The greatest transformation took place on earth two thousand years ago when the Son of God came to earth and revealed to us a new way of living. He demonstrated the lifestyle of the Kingdom of God, but for many His ways were so radical and drastic that unregenerate man could not comprehend or tolerate it. Instead of receiving change and transformation into their hearts they were motivated by that great deceiver, the devil, to kill the Source of true and genuine transformation on a cross. For any seed to bear much fruit, it first has to die and be buried. Little did Satan know when he orchestrated the death of Jesus, that he was actually fulfilling the will of the Father, Jesus being the 'Seed' of *Genesis 3:15* that would crush Satan's head. Jesus had to sacrifice His life, shed His precious blood and pour it on the heavenly altar, becoming the eternal sacrifice for sin once and for all. After His death, He was placed in a tomb and on the third day He rose from the dead. The 'Seed' was now able to bear **much fruit** and Jesus gave His Body, the church, His resurrection power through the rebirth of the spirit of man. Jesus became the first fruit of the resurrection, and we too will need to die daily to this old sinful nature. Only then can we rise to new life in the Spirit, controlled by the Holy Spirit as we renew our minds, training ourselves daily to think like Christ and act like Christ.

By allowing the Kingdom of God to rule in and through our lives, we are ready to become **'transformers'**, changing, impacting and affecting all those lives that surround us. My prayer for you is that you will be transformed in these next 21 days as you allow the Holy Spirit to take control of **every area** of your life.

Through the years that I have been serving the Lord I found myself impacted by the lives of many men and women who have lived **surrendered** lives. They have been such an inspiration and motivation to me, encouraging me to persist and follow their example. Through their lives I discovered that every person who truly desires it, **can live a successful and fulfilled life** on this earth.

Don't Get Sidetracked

In my first book I took believers on a 21-day journey into discovering the King and His Kingdom. Together we grasped the truths of God's Kingdom within us and its transforming power. Next we took a 21-day Prophetic Prayer Journey, and discovered how to enter in beyond the veil of the 'Secret Place'. We learned to pray 'laser-focussed' prayers that would transform our lives and the lives of those around us. This 21-day Spiritual Formation will expose and highlight the areas of our lives that need change so that we can align our spiritual lives with the Spirit of God. The purpose of my books have been to help every child of God hear from the Father more effectively and discover God's purpose for their lives. We have been created to serve our Creator, but we don't always know how best to achieve this goal because our lives are so cluttered with worldly distractions and diversions. There is an ongoing battle of the will and the devil knows that as long as he can keep us sidetracked we will be useless and ineffective in the Kingdom of God.

For 21 days allow the Holy Spirit to take control of your life. He will help you deal with issues that have been clouding your judgement and He will change you from the **inside out**. There is no quick fix or an instant change formula, but the Holy Spirit will take you slowly and deliberately through this transformation, helping you to adjust and even revolutionise your behaviour until it resembles that of our Lord and Saviour, Jesus Christ.

We are 'Earthly Tabernacles'

I have always described our walk with the Lord as a **journey**, for we are in a **process** of being changed into the image of Jesus Christ which will continue until the Lord takes us home to be with Him. On this journey we will discover that our bodies are 'tabernacles' of the Holy Spirit, in other words, a place of dwelling for God's Holy Spirit. Jesus promised in *John 14* that He would sent us a Helper the Holy Spirit to live in us and help and guide us through life. It is therefore our responsibility to align our 'tabernacles' to resemble that of the heavenly tabernacle of God (read the book of Hebrews chapter 9 to understand the heavenly tabernacle also). We will have to make choices and these choices will determine the outcome and end result of this journey on earth. Many will succeed but some will fail and those who fail will have no one to blame but themselves. God said in the book of *Deuteronomy 30:19* that He sets before us blessing and cursing, life and death. We will be foolish not to choose blessing and life, but we will need to LOVE and OBEY the Lord and CLING to Him, embracing His Kingdom rule in our lives. It is in these three capitalised words that the success of our lives on earth and our place in eternity is guaranteed. We must love God to the full, obey Him through total surrender and cling to Him with absolute assurance that He is our Lord, our King and our Master. Jesus 'tabernacled' amongst mankind for three years, just like the Tabernacle which bore the presence of God in the Wilderness and gave us the pattern to imitate. Choose to follow His example, and you will find His power and His blessing in all you do.

Yours in the love of Christ

Harold F. Weitsz

Contents

Contents

Is It Necessary to Fast?

*Matthew 17:14-21 [NKJV] And when they had come to the multitude, a man came to Him, kneeling down to Him and saying, "Lord, have mercy on my son, for he is an epileptic and suffers severely; for he often falls into the fire and often into the water. So I brought him to Your disciples, but they could not cure him." Then Jesus answered and said, "**O faithless and perverse generation,** how long shall I be with you? How long shall I bear with you? Bring him here to Me." And Jesus rebuked the demon, and it came out of him; and the child was cured from that very hour. Then the disciples came to Jesus privately and said, "Why could we not cast it out?" So Jesus said to them, "Because of your unbelief; for assuredly, I say to you, if you have faith as a mustard seed, you will say to this mountain, 'Move from here to there,' and it will move; and nothing will be impossible for you. However, this kind does not go out **except by prayer and fasting**."*

Jesus often referred to the importance of fasting. He emphasised the necessity of fasting, especially when prayer alone could not bring about the desired results as seen in the scripture above. I have often said that fasting with prayer will move the mountains that prayer alone cannot move.

Jesus called His followers a 'faithless and perverse' generation. He was very unimpressed with their **lack of faith**, but He never left them in their state of despair, He gave them a powerful principle that would help them and all future believers to **strengthen their faith** and that was the principle of fasting coupled with prayer.

The Launch Pad Into the Miraculous

Through the years of practising a lifestyle of fasting, I discovered that fasting was like a launch pad for a miraculous walk with God. During periods of fasting I often felt that I didn't want to break the fast because at times I was so caught up in the presence of the Father. It was so precious, yet very fragile and any form of sin or carnality could mar the moment. I felt that my eating would taint the glorious experience, yet I knew I had to move on and do what the Father had instructed me to do.

Fasting causes the physical and spiritual senses to become more sensitive and alert. We become more attentive to our natural surroundings and especially the spiritual world. During these times of separation the Lord has given me visions and dreams, direction for my future and also the faith to flow in the gifts of the Holy Spirit.

We as Christ-followers often forget that we are Kingdom of God citizens and no longer citizens of this world. In *James 4:4* we are told that friendship with this world makes us enemies of God. It often takes times of **fasting, prayer** and **separation** to bring us back to our commitment, restore our faith and re-instill those very important Kingdom values. The world around us is extremely negative and if we do not watch ourselves and do everything spiritually possible to restore or keep our faith levels high, we will get pulled down into the same cauldron of simmering negativity.

God has not given us a spirit of fear, but of **love, power** and a **sound mind** *[2 Timothy 1:7]*. When we are not tuned into the Spirit of God, we can so easily lose our 'Kingdom sanity' which is love, joy, peace, kindness, goodness, faithfulness, gentleness, self-control and long-suffering *[Galatians 5:22-23]*. We must guard against embracing this world's 'sanity'

which ultimately leads to depression, misery and hopelessness.

Praying for Breakthrough

In *Isaiah 58* we see the powerful results that come through
fasting. Jesus also taught the principle of fasting as a lifestyle
for all New Testament believers *[Mark 2:18-21]*. He gave us
a lifeline, knowing that we would all have trials and tribula-
tions and that fasting would be the only way out in certain
instances. I, together with the local church, can vouch for
the wonderful successes and breakthroughs we have experienced through the years as a result of the annual '21-day
Daniel's fast'.

Jesus Deemed it Necessary to Fast

Did you ever stop and think that even our Lord Jesus Christ
deemed it necessary to fast at the beginning of His ministry?
It was only after His 40 day fast that His ministry began. He
returned from the wilderness in the power of the Holy Spirit
and began preaching about the Kingdom of God *[Luke 4:14-
19]*. It was during and at the end of His fast that Jesus broke
all ties with the world. He overcame the three temptations
categorised in *1 John 2:15-16* and this victory gave Him the
power to rule over life and even death. In this example He
demonstrated to us that it is possible to **overcome all of life's
difficulties**.

*1 John 2:15-16 [NLT] Do not love this world nor the things
it offers you, for when you love the world, you do not have
the love of the Father in you. For the world offers only (1)
a craving for physical pleasure, (2) a craving for everything
we see, and (3) pride in our achievements and possessions.
These are not from the Father, but are from this world.*

There is a dimension in fasting that helps us to overcome the lusts and desires of the flesh which must never be overlooked. Fasting can also mean to loosen, for we learn to untie ourselves from the lusts of the flesh and it's various bondages, for example: drug addictions (medications, smoking, alcohol), sexual addictions (pornography, bad movies and unsavoury Internet activities), bad or excessive eating habits and various other works of the flesh as seen in *Galatians 5:19-21*. By resisting and withdrawing from the flesh and its temptations for 21 days, the body and mind 're-programme' themselves to accept a new lifestyle. There is such victory in this exercise, but the important factor is to carefully guard against leaving any doors open that will cause a person to return to old sinful practices.

21-day Daniel's Fast and Various Types of Fasts

For those of you who are going to use this book as part of a time of fasting, it is necessary that you observe the correct fasting procedures. There are various kinds of fasts and the mildest is probably the **21-day Daniel's fast** as described in *Daniel chapters 1 and 10* which consists of fruit, vegetables and nuts. Animal substances like meat, eggs and dairy products must be avoided. Diabetics must carefully monitor their diet to ensure that they receive the necessary foods to sustain their condition.

Pure water fasts can be dangerous if you are on chronic medications. I have personally experienced that a good time of fasting cures many ailments like high blood pressure, cholesterol and many diet-related illnesses. The water fast is very rewarding and I can personally vouch for it, but you need to take time off and focus on the Lord throughout this period.

Short water fasts are very good and can vary from one day a week, to fasting an entire seven days if led by the Holy Spirit. When breaking a water fast after three days or longer, it must be broken with fruit and vegetable juices and never with meat or dairy products. Depending on the duration of the fast, for instance after seven days, one should avoid meat products for at least the first two days, as it causes cramping and stomach pains.

We read of **40-day fasts** in the Bible and they must always be with water and carefully monitored. Breaking this fast with correct food is of utmost importance. Normally you would start with diluted orange juice and carrot juice for the first two or three days and then move on to fruit solids for a few days before bringing meat back into your diet.

You can access material on fasting on our Website at: HAROLDWEITSZ.COM | www.haroldweitsz.com

Week 1

Serving the Father With the Spirit

Week 1

Serving the Father With the Spirit

God gave me a beautiful analogy of the spirit, soul and body of man as seen in the **Tabernacle in the Wilderness**. In this analogy I hope to leave an indelible imprint on your mind and help you discern between the carnal and spiritual man.

In the Old Testament the children of God approached the Lord from the **outside in,** but we as born-again spirit-filled children of God approach Him from the **inside out**.

John 4:23-24 [NKJV] But the hour is coming, and now is, when the true worshipers will **worship the Father in spirit and truth***; for the Father is seeking such to worship Him. God is Spirit, and those who worship Him must worship in spirit and truth.*

In the Old Testament they had the pattern **to the power**, but we have a heavenly deposit of God's supernatural, overcoming power **in our spirits**. In fact, we now have the **content of the power** available to us as revealed in *Colossians 1:26-27*. Every aspect of the tabernacle was a picture of God's intended plan for relationship with man on the earth, and was a replica of what already existed in heaven *[Hebrews 9:23-24]*. There were three areas depicted in the Tabernacle: Firstly the Outer Court which I compare to the flesh dimension for spiritual illustration. It contained the Altar of Sacrifice and the Brazen Laver. The second area was the Holy Place which I refer to as the soul or mind dimension and it housed the Golden Lampstand, the Table of Shewbread and

The Way into the Holy of Holies

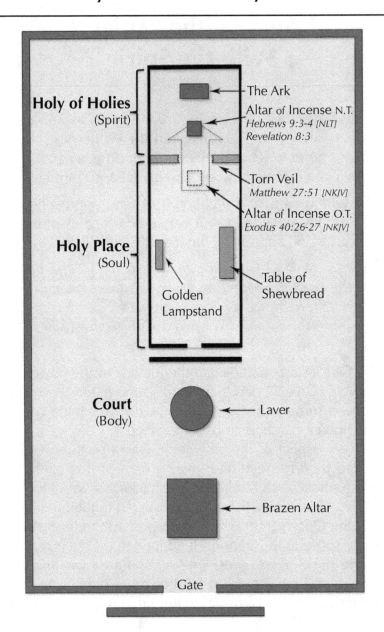

Holy of Holies
(Spirit)

The Ark

Altar of Incense N.T.
Hebrews 9:3-4 [NLT]
Revelation 8:3

Torn Veil
Matthew 27:51 [NKJV]

Altar of Incense O.T.
Exodus 40:26-27 [NKJV]

Holy Place
(Soul)

Golden
Lampstand

Table of
Shewbread

Court
(Body)

Laver

Brazen Altar

Gate

the Altar of Incense. The last and most revered area was the Holy of Holies which resembles the spirit or heart of man where the Holy Spirit lives. It was in the Holy of Holies that the Mercy Seat and Ark of the Covenant were housed and was the meeting place of God in the Wilderness. In Day 21, I will elaborate more fully on these aspects of the Tabernacle.

In this week's sessions I was very tempted to start with the aspects of the outer court, but I realised that unless we had a full revelation of our **spiritual salvation** we would not be able to deal with the soul and the flesh successfully. The reason why so many Christians are battling in life is because they do not realise the great price of their salvation. They in turn must manifest this salvation through godly conduct with fear and deep reverence towards the Father. The Holy Spirit convicts us in our spirits first and then we act with our minds and our bodies. In *1 Thessalonians 5:23* we read that we are spirit, soul and body, but not everyone has a revelation of how these three elements operate within the structure and make-up of God's created being.

We worship the Father with our spirits, but we must train our minds and bodies to worship Him as well. To do this successfully we have to understand the spiritual journey Christ demonstrated for us through His life on earth. He gave us a full, living demonstration of the pattern to the power.

Philippians 2:12-13 [NLT] Work hard to show the results of your salvation, obeying God with deep reverence and fear. For God is working in you, giving you the desire and the power to do what pleases Him.

Day 1
Spiritual Poverty

Matthew 5:3 [NLT] God blesses those who are poor and realize their need for Him, for the Kingdom of Heaven is theirs.

On Day 1, reassess your spiritual condition. This is a very necessary **daily** exercise which brings us to the feet of our Lord, as we enter His presence with hearts ready to do His will. In our 21-day journey we will be addressing the three areas of the tabernacle, namely the Outer Court, the Holy Place and the Holy of Holies. I don't want to remain in the Outer Court, but I want to press on, into the Holy Place and finally beyond the veil into the Holy of Holies where my Father dwells and is waiting for me.

The reason that many Christians do not press in beyond the veil is because they have so many 'cluttered' and sinful areas in their lives and do not know how to 'unclog' the spiritual channel to the Father. There is a spiritual drought and poverty in the Body of Christ that needs to be addressed before we can experience the fullness that the Father has reserved for His children. Every day we need to approach God's throne of grace with a deep humility and a heart that is exposed and laid bare before our Father. We only realise our lack and need when we **judge our lives against the backdrop of Christ's sacrifice.** There can be no pride be it of person, place, position or race when we are confronted with the life and person of Jesus. We need to realise our desperately sorry state and turn to the Lord with no **reservations, conditions or distractions.**

What Should Our Highest Goal Be?

This is such an interesting question to ask any Christian and I am sure you will hear many answers. Before you read my answer, ask yourself this question, "what is my highest goal?" It is a known fact that without a goal there can be no direction or purpose in life. The treatment of ailments resulting directly from depression and stress are recorded as the highest claims by medical aids. I believe with all my heart that the cause for all this is found in the spiritual dimension and this is the crux of *Matthew 6:33*. One of the reasons for depression and stress in society is that people are so caught up in the here and now, trying to keeping up with the unreasonable and ungodly work pace and other commitments. Many have lost sight of their goal and purpose because of wrong values. When we place the Kingdom of God at the centre of our value system we will discover our goal and purpose.

Our highest goal is found in *Matthew 6:33* where Jesus clearly instructs believers to **SEEK FIRST the Kingdom** of God. A kingdom must have a king and he is the focal point of the kingdom. Without a Queen, Britain would have no purpose or value in Buckingham Palace except historical value, where once upon a time there lived a royal family. Jesus, by pointing to the Kingdom of God, was directly pointing to Himself as the King of kings. Prior to His crucifixion, many in Israel recognised and realised that He was the Messiah and they hailed Him as such as He rode into Jerusalem on a donkey *[Matthew 21]*.

The highest goal becomes clearer when the Apostle Paul in *Romans 8:29* tells us that we were **predestined to be transformed** into the image of Christ. Christ-likeness becomes our highest goal. We have a choice to either be **conformed** to this world or be **transformed** by the renewing of our minds and start resembling and imitating our Lord and Saviour, Jesus Christ *[Romans 12:1-2]*.

Redeemed from a Calamitous Eternal State

We must come to a deep and lasting understanding of the sacrifice of Jesus and the finished work of the cross. I have been instrumental in seeing so many people receive Jesus as their Saviour, but have not seen many reach the full depth and understanding of His great sacrifice. Our spiritual poverty was immeasurable and we were in a state of spiritual death. There was **nothing** we could do to get ourselves out of this calamitous, eternal state.

Romans 5:10-11 [NLT] For since our friendship with God was restored by the death of His Son while we were still His enemies, we will certainly be saved through the life of His Son.

The realization of just how disastrous our spiritual state was is seen in the above scripture. We were enemies of our Creator *[Romans 5:9-10; Colossians 1:21-23]*. Through sin and rebellion mankind separated itself from God and His Kingdom. Because of the Father-heart of God, He could not leave His precious creation in that state forever, so He sent His Son to this earth in the form of a man to take all our sin upon Himself. He died on the altar of sacrifice (the cross), shed His blood and redeemed us from eternal death and separation from Him.

Don't Trade with God's Eternal Gift

*Hebrews 12:16 [Message] Watch out for the **Esau syndrome**: trading away God's lifelong gift in order to satisfy a short-term appetite.*

I find the example of Esau and Jacob so fitting. We see two men with two vastly different perspectives. Esau had **no spiritual discernment of eternal values;** he only lived for the here and now. Esau can be compared to people who have heard of the Lord, but have never sought an encounter with the living God. Their values stretch as far as their perception of eternity. Jacob on the other hand realised the eternal value of the blessing, but he used deceptive means to acquire it. He thought he could bribe and cheat his way into receiving eternal blessings. Jacob knew that there was great value in obtaining the birthright, but he went about devious means to obtain it. He never received the birthright because he deserved it, but simply because Esau despised it. Many Christians are like this. They know that there is value in being a Christian, but they are not prepared to pay the price and live surrendered lives, as a result they never obtain the full measure of blessing that God has for them. Many believers think they can serve the Lord in a cheap half-hearted fashion, not realising their spiritual poverty and only making time for the Lord here and there in their busy schedules. I call it the 'I'll do it my way' syndrome and the Message Bible calls it the 'Esau syndrome'.

Identification and Acknowledgement

First and foremost, **identify and acknowledge sin areas** in your life. Do not go into denial or you will never experience God's spiritual freedom or wealth for your life. If Jacob had only been honest with himself he would never have had to go through the hardship of working so long under his uncle Laban who was a very divisive and deceptive man. I am sure that through the years Jacob came to see himself and his own deceptive character mirrored the life of his uncle Laban. It took Jacob over 21 years to free himself from the yoke of bondage because of his own deceptive ways. God had to bring Jacob face to face with his ugly self and the way God chose to do so, was through the unrighteous Laban.

Spiritual depth or shallow commitment can be measured by the **visible fruit** in a person's day-to-day life. *John 15:8 [NLT] When you produce much fruit, you are My true disciples. This brings great glory to My Father.*

Make a spiritual evaluation of your life today and re-commit your life to God so that you can experience the promise behind *Matthew 6:33 [NLT] Seek the Kingdom of God above all else, and live righteously, and **He will give you everything you need.***

Day 2
Spiritual Revolution

---

1 Peter 2:11 [AMP] *Beloved, I implore you as aliens and strangers and exiles [in this world] to abstain from the sensual urges (the evil desires, the passions of the flesh, your lower nature) that wage war against the soul.*

Galatians 5:17 [NLT] *The sinful nature wants to do evil, which is just the opposite of what the Spirit wants. And the Spirit gives us desires that are the opposite of what the sinful nature desires. These two forces are constantly fighting each other, so you are not free to carry out your good intentions.*

I want to paint a picture that will tell a little story giving you insight into the spiritual revolution a person goes through at the point of salvation. We receive salvation in our spirit, but there is a continuous war being waged in our soul and flesh.

There was a body called Flesh who ruled as king over a mind called Soul. Together they were served by a slave called Spirit. Spirit like any other slave had no will of his own and had to serve every whim and urge of the Flesh, to put it more bluntly Spirit was 'enslaved' to Flesh. Soul on the other hand was a servant and had a mind of his own from time to time. Although a servant, Soul had more freedom than Spirit, but was negatively impacted by the impulses and negative behaviour of Flesh, even though he knew that Flesh's behaviour was wrong. Soul knew deep down of right and wrong, but he had no control over the vices of Flesh and was compelled to serve him most times.

There came a time when a supernatural event (rebirth) took

place and Flesh was demoted to the position of a slave, while 'reborn' Spirit became the king. This caused such a chaotic situation in the life of Flesh that till today he still tries to create insurgency and rebellion against Spirit. Soul on the other hand is constantly at war within himself, because he was so programmed to serving Flesh in all his lusts and wrong desires. Soul continually has to make 180^0 adjustments to re-programme his thinking and wipe out past memories and bad habits.

In this little story I have sketched a picture of the inward battle that rages in the life of every born again man and woman. When we understand the change that took place when we were born-again, we begin to progress spiritually and walk in victory in our thoughts and actions.

Are You Ready?

Are you ready to break out of this sin riddled, sin racked world? Are you ready to overthrow the soulish revolution at war within your members? Revolutions through the centuries have brought about national and many times worldwide changes of which some have been good and beneficial to mankind. Martin Luther changed the church world forever when he grasped the revelation of the truth that 'the just shall live by faith'. He caused a major revolution within the Catholic institution that at the time relied on indulgence money as a major source of revenue. They based their cause on the false doctrine that freedom from punishment of sin and forgiveness could only be bought by the purchasing of 'indulgences' and this would spare the sinner time in purgatory. Purgatory is a fictitious place of fire where souls are supposed to remain until they have supposedly paid for their sins and then are free to go to heaven. This brought about the worldwide shift from Catholicism to Protantism and the world entered into a new and liberating spiritual awakening.

I hope to help you enter a new and liberating chapter in your spiritual life, if you are not already there. It is essential that you confront and purge all worldliness that defiles and contaminates your soul. I wish to bring about a revolt in your heart against sin and unrighteous living.

This revolution is going to cost you, so please do not cringe at the thought of the word 'loss' and lose me on this point! There are things we need to lose, there are things we need to bid farewell to forever, so that we can walk in the freedom of God's love and grace in this very 'un-free' and troubled world.

Lose the Old Nature

We need to lose the ugly old self, selfishness, and the self-centredness. Our old nature when seen and measured against the light of God's Word has been so difficult for us to live with and also difficult for others to live with, but most importantly, impossible for our Heavenly Father to accept or approve. I see so many Christians grappling and struggling with the idea of surrender. I know this to be a fact for I was there myself until I took the huge step and started the process of **intentional surrender**. Believe me, I have by no means arrived, but I am on a **daily course of action**, surrendering to the will of the Father as the Holy Spirit reveals to me a far better and successful way to live.

A Revolution Called 'The Way'

'The Way' was the name that the Early church in Jerusalem was known by. They were marked by their radical and revolutionary lifestyle. They had something profound and the Jewish world was torn between accepting this newfound

'Way' or totally rejecting it. This is what a revolution does; it revolts against the institutions and traditions of what mankind has been accustomed to and comfortable with. Inherent in every person is a **deep-seated knowledge of right and wrong**. Remember we have been made in the image and likeness of God and His DNA is in the very fibre of our beings. When God breathed into man the breath of life *[Genesis 2:7]*, it was His life, His creative ability that man received. We can therefore say that we have the life of God inside us. He is the Creator of all life and through His Spirit He is drawing us back to Himself.

This process of drawing us back is what causes a revolution in our soul and our flesh. The Apostle Paul so aptly describes the war in our sinful nature as the flesh that is permanently opposing the way of the spirit *[Galatians 5:16-17]*. This war brings great discomfort and displeasure to the flesh which continuously resists the new lifestyle that EVERY child of God must enter into.

Satan is a liar and deceiver and if we do not make a huge spiritual effort with the help of God's Holy Spirit to turn our backs on the works of the flesh, we will not succeed in truly overcoming this world and its deceptive attractions. Everything in this world is geared to drawing us away from Jesus and His Kingdom. The Father wants us to have a good life and His original plan and intention was that we would serve Him with all our hearts and live life to the full on this planet that He created for us. It is up to us to make a clear distinction between wanting what He wants for us and wanting what Satan knows will destroy us. That is why it is so important to be fully submitted and surrendered to Him so that we can find His will and His purposes for our lives.

Daily Spiritual Exercise

This is always the difficult part of this 21-day journey, where you must make an honest assessment of your life. It is natural to resist change, for change can be painful and downright uncomfortable at first. But let me assure you that the rewards are liberating and very therapeutic, in fact it can be compared to a visit to the doctor for some or other ailment. At first you feel terrible, but when the medication kicks in, you experience a time of relief and wellness as the body responds to treatment.

Write down your daily thoughts and experiences as the Lord assists you through these 21 days. Write down what areas in your life need a spiritual revolution so that you can walk in God's fullness.

Day 3
Spiritual Transformation

*Matthew 3:2 [AMP] Repent (**think** differently; **change** your mind, **regretting** your sins and **changing** your conduct), for the kingdom of heaven is at hand.*

In our study today I want you to imagine the site on the banks of the River Jordan two thousand years ago where a baptismal service was taking place. It was a strange scene and there was a strange man called John the Baptist. The message that John preached was 'Come and REPENT for the Kingdom of God is at hand' *[Matthew 3:2]*. John, by worldly standards, was wild, unkept and socially un-presentable. He lived on locusts and honey and wore a crude garment made of camel's hair. Nothing about his external appearance could hide his love for God and his conviction of sin. Many who heard him were drawn to this zealous follower of God. His message was radical, challenging and even offensive to many whose hearts remained hardened. By social standing, he was nothing to aspire to, yet thousands came to hear him and many converts were baptised.

Among the believers were some rather sceptical Pharisees and Sadducees who regarded themselves as 'God's chosen ones'. In their hearts they KNEW there was something lacking in their lives, so fearing that they might miss out on some or other experience, they came to be baptised by the prophet. John saw through their guise and to quote from the Message Bible he firmly rebuked them saying *"Brood of snakes! What do you think you're doing slithering down here to the river? Do you think a little water on your snake skins is going* *to make any difference? It's **your life that must change**, not your skin!" [**Matthew 3:7-8**].* This scathing remark, exposed the religious system of many of Israel's spiritual leaders.

An Inner Revelation

I personally do not know of a single person who does not have a desire to be a better person. The problem however arises for many when they fail to understand that all change must start on the **inside** and then manifest in words and actions on the **outside**. If change is only brought about in our outward behaviour, it cannot last because through our own human strength we cannot control the lusts and desires of the flesh. It is only through the power of the Holy Spirit living on the inside of us, helping and guiding us, that we can have any lasting success. I desire with all my heart to show you a new way of living that will so change your way of thinking and doing that you will be transformed into 'another man', a 'new person'.

1 Samuel 10:6 [Message] Before you know it, the Spirit of God will come on you and you'll be transformed. You'll be a new person!

Only a Transformed Person can Bring About Transformation

Transformation has become a cliché in the political arena where politicians and world leaders use this word constantly to create expectation in the hearts of people who are looking to them for change in this messed up, chaotic world. The truth of the matter is that only a Spirit-filled child of God can truly bring about transformation, the reason being that there is only one 'Transformer' in all this universe and His name is Jesus. When a person is surrendered to God, then the Lord can use this person to bring about life-changing, situation-changing transformation.

The only real and lasting transformation is an **inner spiritual transformation**. The mind and the flesh **cannot** have any lasting change without the spirit being re-born *[John 3:3]*. Unless a man be born again of the Spirit of God he cannot experience any lasting transformation. Nicodemus, a Pharisee in the Bible, was a man deeply committed to God and desperate for change. By observing Jesus he had come to realise that in himself he could not change and the law that he had studied all his life could not change him either. He finally scraped up the courage to approach Jesus and ask how he too could have this spiritual power. He realised that out of Jesus flowed the source of all truth and revelation and he desperately needed that. Nicodemus **saw the power and love of God** in operation in the life of Jesus and he had to find the key to spiritual well-being and eternal life *[John 3:1-18; John 14:6-7]*.

God has to work from the inside out and there can be no half measures. It's all or nothing and that is why surrender is the **key action**. Please note I said **key action** and not **key word**. We can say a lot and have the best intentions, but only actions will produce the fruit of a truly victorious life in the Spirit. The Message Bible gives us a straight and clear direction without mincing any words:

*Romans 12:1-2 [Message] So here's what I want you to do, God helping you: Take your everyday, ordinary life — your sleeping, eating, going-to-work, and walking-around life — and **place it before God as an offering**. Embracing what God does for you is the best thing you can do for Him. **Don't become so well-adjusted to your culture that you fit into it without even thinking.** Instead, fix your attention on God.*

You'll be changed from the inside out. Readily recognize what He wants from you, and quickly respond to it. Unlike the culture around you, always dragging you down to its level of immaturity, God brings the best out of you, develops well-formed maturity in you.

Discovering the Kingdom Within You

No one in absolute honesty before God can say "I am satisfied with the person I am on the inside" except those who have accepted the Kingdom into their hearts and are in a **daily lifelong process of change**. The snag for many though is the understanding and coming to terms with the 'Kingdom of God'. The 'Kingdom' was a very strange and foreign term that Jesus used and it speaks of entering into another world, another dimension of life. Our daily scripture *[Matthew 3:2]* highlights three characteristics of the person who has been born again. This person has entered into the Kingdom and is undergoing a **character change**.

1. Firstly such a person begins to THINK differently because he now has the Mind of Christ *[Philippians 2:5]*. The Word clearly states that when we are in Christ, we no longer live but Christ now lives in us. As we surrender to His Kingdom, we are able to tune into **His thoughts** and **His voice** in our spirits *[Galatians 2:20]*.

2. Secondly this person ACTS differently resulting from **repentance and remorse** of past sins. I once heard somebody say that great repentance is followed by great change. There can be no room for self-justification, for no person was ever worthy or great enough to save themselves. Christ's gift of salvation was beyond measure, therefore our gratitude and appreciation must be beyond measure.

3. True repentance is reflected in a total CHANGE OF CON-DUCT. **Genuine salvation is measured by change and fruit**. I know many people who call themselves Christians, but their conduct remains unchanged. That is why I love the term **Christ-follower** for it speaks of a person whose goal is to become **Christ-like**. You can always SEE when a person has been with Jesus, such a person acts and even speaks like Him. There can be no room for compromise, so when we slip and fall, there must be quick repentance and a return to Kingdom behaviour.

Becoming a
Spiritual 'Transformer'

- Do you have a vision for transformation? Write down your vision, highlighting areas that you know need change. It might mean changing the company you keep, the music you listen to, the movies you watch and the books and magazines you read. Allow the Holy Spirit to work inside of you and repent of all unsurrendered areas.

- What will transformation in your life mean to your family, friends and co-workers? This can be a very liberating spiritual journey, so don't lose heart and never give up.

Day 4
A Spiritually Integrated Person

2 Timothy 3:16-17 [NLT] **All Scripture** *is inspired by God and is useful to teach us what is true and to* **make us realize what is wrong in our lives***. It corrects us when we are wrong and teaches us to do what is right. God uses it to* **prepare and equip** *His people to do every good work.*

The purpose of ALL SCRIPTURE is to correct us, teach us and guide us. As little children the Father expects all parents (whether they do it or not) to raise and instruct their children in how to operate and function in this world in a godly and orderly way. This is the preparation that will train a child to cope with the issues of life. When this very important aspect of growing up is not fulfilled, children end up ill-equipped and dysfunctional, unable to deal with life. This opens the door for Satan to step in and redirect their young lives.

Today's scripture may sound like a mouthful but there must always be a constant desire in our hearts to **change and correct what is wrong**. We must be in constant 'change mode' so that we can grow into fully developed and 'integrated' believers, filled with the wisdom of God and having the Mind of Christ. There is such a cry for mature and balanced Christ-followers, ready to be a model and mentor their children, and also their brothers and sisters in Christ who are battling to survive in life. Jesus showed us a better life, a 'higher-life' that supersedes this 'lower-life' worldly dimension, but we have to deal with our 'lower-life' attitude before we can make the transition.

What is Spiritual Integration?

Colossians 1:28 [AMP] Him we preach and proclaim, warning and admonishing everyone and instructing everyone in all wisdom (comprehensive insight into the ways and purposes of God), that we may present **every person mature** *(full-grown, fully initiated, complete, and perfect) in Christ (the Anointed One).*

'Integrity' forms the root word from which the word 'integrated' is derived. It is a word the world no longer seems to honour or even understand. **Integrity means wholeness** which is a state of **being complete and undivided.** In other words there is no room for compromise or double standards in the life of an integrated person. A spiritually sound and 'whole' person is balanced in his reasoning and is able to remain uninfluenced by corrupt society and its foreign lifestyle and culture. **An integrated person is a Kingdom-minded person.** There is a saying that has taken on a very derogatory meaning, when it should in fact be viewed in a very positive light. The saying goes "a person must never be too heavenly minded or they will be of no earthly use". Lets shed some positive light by changing the sentence and highlighting its true value "a person **must** be heavenly minded so that they can be of **great earthly use**". The truth of the matter is that only a heavenly minded person, filled with God's wisdom can overcome the trials and temptations this world has to offer. A Kingdom-minded person has the ability to hear the voice of God and therefore do the works of God. Jesus was 100% Kingdom-minded. The key is to change our mindset. *Colossians 3:2 [AMP] And* **set your minds and keep them set on what is above** *(the higher things), not on the things that are on the earth.* The Message Bible tells us to, *"pursue the things over which Christ presides. Don't shuffle along, eyes* *to the ground, absorbed with the things right in front of you. Look up, and be alert to what is going on around Christ — that's where the action is. See things from His perspective"*. From this scripture we can gather that the only perspective to have is a Kingdom-minded perspective.

God is our Creator and therefore has the **answers and solutions to all life's problems**. If you truly believe this then you will agree with me that we need to be heavenly-minded in order to be of any earthly use to ourselves and to others.

A Strong Cord

'INTEGRATED' is a buzz word in the market place today, but I am focussing on the spiritual world which supersedes all earthly dimensions. There are three areas that make up a spiritually integrated person. *Ecclesiastes 4:12* tells us that a triple-braided cord cannot be easily broken. In order for us to function as fully integrated Christ-followers we need three elements to hold us together spiritually:

1. There has to be a vibrant, **daily Relationship** with the Father.
2. There has to be a **consistent intake of the Word** of God.
3. There has to be constant **contact and involvement** with the Body of Christ.

Our relationship with the Father enables us to find His will for our lives. We are able to consult Him daily, anytime, anywhere. Through daily study of the Word we are able to discern His voice and refresh ourselves through the washing of water by the Word *[Ephesians 5:26]*. An integrated person will never feel alone or deserted because of the constant contact and communion with other believers. Being connected to the Body of Christ is vital and offers protection, encouragement and accountability. We were never created to live alone. These three elements **working together** build strong character and maturity in a believer. When godly values are intertwined with a person's lifestyle, he starts resembling the person of Christ and Christ's character becomes formed in him. **This is transformation in action.**

'Unclog' the Blocked Channels

The only way that you are going to 'unclog' your mind is by allowing the Holy Spirit to help you **renew your thoughts and attitude** through the study of the Word. With the power of the Holy Spirit we are able to **put on a new nature**, the Christ-like nature. You can choose the way you think and 'Kingdom thinking' means to purposefully, consciously reject negative thoughts that don't line up with the Word of God. No amount of counsel or human effort can bring about such a miracle, only the Holy Spirit can do this *[Ephesians 4:23-24]*.

A spiritually integrated person, in layman's terms, is a person who is applying God's required disciplines in all of his daily living. This process enables a person to become spiritually tuned into hearing from the Father and subsequently doing His will. Through leading a **disciplined thought life** a person will learn to 'unclog' the old blocked channels, remove the clutter and hindrances and start hearing the voice of God speaking through His Word, through circumstances, through other people or in dreams and visions. These are just some of the ways the Lord communicates to His children. This process is a very liberating and rewarding exercise and literally takes a person who has been living the 'lower-life' to the dimension of the 'higher-life' foundation or as my dear friend Dr. Ralph W. Neighbour says, "We become upstairs 'higher-life' people and not downstairs 'lower-life' people."

Jesus was the most integrated person who walked the face of the earth. We can reason and say that it is impossible to become like Him and I would agree, was it not for the indwelling presence of the Holy Spirit who has made it **absolutely possible**. The Bible tells us that the Holy Spirit is the Spirit of Truth *[John 14:17]* and **He will lead and guide us into truth**. In Day 5 I will be dealing with the importance of Truth and its liberating effect on our lives.

Alive to God's Kingdom

I don't know about you, but I want to live in the Kingdom here and now. I want to experience the blessings of the Kingdom but most of all, I want to KNOW the King of the Kingdom. The only way that I can successfully achieve this is by surrendering to the necessary disciplines of the Kingdom in my life. By submitting and yielding to the desires of our flesh and soul we have sold out to the world and its devilish dictates. It's time to reclaim our freedom and discover a new life.

Integrating God's Truths Into Our Lives

Always revisit the biblical basics. Biblical basics are the foundation blocks on which we build our spiritual lives. I mentioned the *three* basics of a spiritually integrated person and unless we strive to maintain these three elements we cannot progress any further in our spiritual walk with the Lord.

- What daily changes would you need to make to improve your *Relationship with the Father?*

- Seek ways to improve your *Word Intake* because this will improve your daily guidance from the Father.

- Finally, how can you improve your relationship with the *Body of Christ?* When you view your fellow brothers and sisters as *Christ's body* you will have a whole new revelation of the function and role you have to play within the community of God's children and the world outside.

May God bless you today and give you a very special day as you meditate on His Word and pray continuously.

Day 5
The Spirit of Truth

*John 8:44 [NLT] He [the devil] was a murderer from the beginning. He has always hated the truth, because there is **no truth in him**. When he lies, it is consistent with his character; for he is a liar and the **father of lies**.*

*Ephesians 2:1-2 [AMP] And you [He made alive], when you were dead (slain) by [your] trespasses and sins in which at one time you walked [habitually]. You were following the course and fashion of this world [were under the sway of the tendency of this present age], following the prince of the power of the air. **You were obedient to and under the control of the [demon] spirit** that still constantly works in the sons of disobedience [the careless, the rebellious, and the unbelieving, who go against the purposes of God].*

It's very hard for some to accept that **we were under the power of Satan and his demons** when we did not have salvation, but we cannot refute the Word for it is TRUTH. If we can accept God's truth, then we can begin to walk in the Spirit of Truth and be led by the Holy Spirit of Truth. When I speak of truth, I am referring to Biblical truth. There is no truth outside of the Word of God and as you have read, Satan and this world system can only produce lies and deception. We are in a tug-of-war with the Holy Spirit at one end and Satan on the other. As we **choose truth**, we move closer to the Lord and He draws closer to us and He reveals His incredible love and grace. This **love is the driving force of His Kingdom** and He releases in us the inspiration to do His will. By not surrendering our lives daily to the Lord we move away from truth and if we are not careful we will again get caught in Satan's web of lies and deception. It is only in the power of the Holy Spirit that we can **discern between truth and lies** and the more Word we take in the more Light and Truth we walk in.

If we could see into the spiritual dimension, we would be shocked to see that many Christians still have one foot in the world and the other foot in the Kingdom of God. I once used the analogy of a **dual passport**. Many people possess dual passports which can be very beneficial when they want to pose as citizens of another nation in order to get the benefits of both countries. Well this may work in the world but the wheels are sure to come off when we apply this modus operandi as Kingdom of God citizens. We cannot be citizens of the Kingdom and still play in the world. These two worlds are at extreme ends of the pendulum and Christians put their lives in serious spiritual danger when they compromise.

Compromise Versus Confrontation

Compromise in Kingdom terms is when Christians take the Truth of God's Word, water it down, and change it to accommodate their sinful lifestyles under the banner of so called 'grace'. **Compromise clearly divides** the nominal (in name only) Christian from the true Christ-follower. **The antonym for compromise is confrontation** and is precisely what the Word of God does in our lives. It confronts every wrong value that is contrary to the Truth. Jesus had to go to the cross, He could not reason with the Father around the only sacrifice that was acceptable to save the whole world. God had given the pattern of sacrifice in the Old Testament that would foreshadow the final sacrifice. Without the shedding of blood there could be no remission for sin. Jesus was the final LAMB and His pure, untainted blood was the only acceptable blood needed to take AWAY the sin of the world. He had to bear the pain and suffering of the world. Jesus who knew no sin, took upon His body our sin and sickness, He was despised by man and finally rejected by His Father because of our sin. All this had to happen so that He could set us free and give us back eternal life with the Father. I often wondered why the Father turned His back on His only Son when He hung on the cross, until I realised that it was the world's sin and sickness that reviled the Father even though He was heartbroken for His Son *[2 Corinthians 5:21]*. Once His blood was shed and the sin removed, Jesus rose from the dead and stood before the Father as the 'first born from the dead'. The blood of Jesus washed away our unrighteousness, making us righteous and through this action brought us back into fellowship with the Father through the 'veil of His flesh' *[Hebrews 10:19-20]*.

No Truth - No Power

For Truth to prevail and have power, all untruth and falsehood in our lives have to be **exposed and acknowledged**. Often the hardest truth is to really perceive ourselves as God perceives us. It is our sin nature that wants to hide sin and sweep it under the proverbial carpet, but the Father sees and knows all, that is why Jesus said that we will know the Truth, and the Truth will set us free. We know truth through the conviction of the Holy Spirit working on the inside of us, guiding us to clean out our lives and preparing us to walk in the fullness of God's revelation and knowledge.

There is tremendous freedom in truth, even though there are consequences for the wrongs we have done. Truth throws us into the merciful arms of God and empowers Him to bring about a grace-filled deliverance. We are deceived if we assume that we can water down God's Truth with a compromised lifestyle and think it is acceptable to a holy and un-compromising God. The spirit is willing but the flesh is weak and no person wants to leave their comfort zone. Unfortunately we have no choice if we want to experience true and lasting success in life *[Matthew 26:41]*. I once preached a message that Christ rules from the cross and we too can only successfully rule over life and its problems 'from the cross' by crucifying the flesh. It's on the cross that Jesus took back all power from the enemy and it is on the cross spiritually that we will receive the power to overcome in this world with the help of the Holy Spirit.

When we compromise any truth in God's Word we deny the cross and render the Word ineffective, causing it to lose its power. For example: ***Ephesians 2:13*** *[NKJV] But now in Christ Jesus you who once were far off have been brought near by **the blood of Christ**.*

If we were to take the blood out of this verse and replace it with the death of Jesus, the power that is in the emphasis on the blood would be lost. It was not His death that gave us the victory, but His blood *[Hebrews 9:12]*. His blood was untainted by sin and had to be poured out over the heavenly mercy seat in order to purchase the freedom of mankind. If Jesus only died and never took His blood to the mercy seat there would have been no forgiveness of sin *[Leviticus 16:14-15]*.

Political leaders have ignored God's truth and have tailored legislation like a suit of clothing to fit the sinful lifestyles of their nation's citizens. What they do not realise is that they are building on sands of compromise and this forms an un-stable foundation, believing it will bring peace and unity and be beneficial to all. Yes! It does bring about peace, **a pseu-do peace**, creating false hope and temporary solutions but like the house built on sand, when the storms come and the winds blow there is no foundation to uphold it and it crumbles and disappears. Only a foundation of Truth based on the principles and values of God's Word can take us safely through the storms.

We are dealing with the Spirit of Truth and this especially extends to the business world. Many believers fall into the trap of reasoning that it is the acceptable norm to compromise, for after all this is how the world operates and it works. The deception is that it does work, but only for a while for **anything that is not built on Kingdom principles WILL ultimately fail.** Nations whose roots were once laid on sound biblical values are reeling today under the weight of compromising politicians. Pillars of morality and sound ethics which for years were the preservation of nations have been compromised and even destroyed. What was once called evil is now called good, and what was good is now called evil [Isaiah 5:20]. **Whatever is upheld that is contrary to the Kingdom values will ultimately be lost.**

A person who aspires to be a spiritually integrated person **cannot** afford compromise. Compromise will surely draw us back into the world and we will ultimately experience spiritual, personal and relational loss. I always compare compromise to someone who is standing on a table and is trying to pull another up alongside of him. The odds of success are against him for he will eventually get pulled down and suffer great loss in the following three areas: **Spiritually**; he will lose God's blessing and guidance. **Personally**; he will go against his conscience and there will be no lasting joy. **Relational**; it will affect his relationship with the Lord and those around him. Do not be deceived you cannot have any lasting success without total surrender to the King and His Kingdom.

The Truth Shall Set You Free

For God to be real to us, we have to be **real and truthful** to ourselves. In *John 8:32* we read very clearly that we can only be true and genuine Christ-followers if we **abide in His Word** and **walk in Truth**. We have to take a long hard look at our lives and the way we are living from day-to-day. I am always amazed at how many Christians can live their lives oblivious of the fact that **the Holy Spirit is living on the inside of them**. They continue to walk in sinful ways and I can only come to the conclusion that they have not truly been born-again of the Spirit.

Nurture Truth

If we, for the purpose of illustration, could personify Truth and see it as a small infant, how will we set about caring for it? A caring mother will nurture, care and give it all her love and attention. Ultimately the infant will grow and blossom under such love and care. This is exactly what will happen if we take hold of the Spirit of Truth and embrace it as part of our spirit, soul and body. What do you think will be the outcome? Firstly God's Word tells us that **we will be set free**. Free from the chains of bondage that Satan has held us captive with all these years. Free from the vice-grip of sin. Free from this world and all its filth and enticements. Free to serve God with everything within us.

Establishing Integrity
In All Areas

Today's exercise must be tackled with honesty, frankness and deep sincerity. Each one of us needs to regularly make an honest assessment of every wrong or compromised area in our lives. The purpose of this exercise is to remove any area that will keep you from entering into the presence of the Father.

No matter how hard, we have **to truthfully examine our lives**, eradicate all lies and falsehood and root out sin. Hearts can be compared to vegetable gardens. There are many vegetables that are good to eat, but the weeds that have not been plucked out will eventually multiply and strangle the good food in between. We cannot give more fertilizer (the Word) and hope the weeds will eventually disappear. We have to uproot sin or we will never come to a place where we can have unbroken fellowship with the Father.

I strongly believe that the lack of honesty and truth in our lives is one of the greatest hindrances, preventing us from entering into a loving and fulfilling relationship with the Father.

Day 6
Spiritual Wisdom and Insight

*1 Corinthians 1:18-25 [NLT] The message of the cross is foolish to those who are headed for destruction! But we who are being saved know it is the very power of God. As the Scriptures say, "I will destroy the **wisdom of the wise** and discard the intelligence of the intelligent." So where does this leave the philosophers, the scholars, and the world's brilliant debaters? God has made the **wisdom** of this world look foolish. Since God in His **wisdom** saw to it that the world would never know Him through human **wisdom**, He has used our foolish preaching to save those who believe. It is foolish to the Jews, who ask for signs from heaven. And it is foolish to the Greeks, who seek human **wisdom**. So when we preach that Christ was crucified, the Jews are offended and the Gentiles say it's all nonsense. But to those called by God to salvation, both Jews and Gentiles, **Christ is the power of God and the wisdom of God**. This foolish plan of God is wiser than the wisest of human plans, and God's weakness is stronger than the greatest of human strength.*

Six times in this scripture we read of wisdom, what it is and is not. The Father knows that without wisdom, knowledge and insight we will not survive the many pitfalls and snares of the enemy in this world. In verse 24 we read that Jesus is the manifestation and the sum total of the Father's wisdom in the flesh. Jesus came and revealed the Father to mankind through **His words** and **actions**. Jesus revealed the true essence of LIFE by showing mankind **a new way of living**, led and inspired by the Holy Spirit. My simple layman's definition of godly wisdom is (1) KNOWING GOD'S TRUTH (the Word) and (2) LIVING it. These two elements **cannot be separated** from one another. We can read God's Word and know it from beginning to end, but by not applying it and living it, it will only amount to wonderful head knowledge.

A Call to Character

*Mark 4:15-20 [Message] Some people are like the seed that falls on the **hardened soil** of the road. No sooner do they hear the Word than **Satan snatches away** what has been planted in them. And some are like the seed that lands in the **gravel**. When they first hear the Word, they respond with great enthusiasm. But there is such **shallow soil of character** that when the emotions wear off and some difficulty arrives, there is nothing to show for it. The seed cast in the **weeds** represents the ones who hear the kingdom news but are **overwhelmed with worries** about all the things they have to do and all the things they want to get. The **stress strangles what they heard**, and nothing comes of it. But the seed planted in the **good earth** represents those who hear the Word, embrace it, and **produce a harvest** beyond their wildest dreams.*

This scripture depicts those who discover God's wisdom. Some grasp it, hold onto it and discover true life, while others, lacking strength of character, are unable to follow through and remain defeated by life's circumstances.

Spiritual wisdom and insight are directly linked to the character of man. These attributes have to be developed, they are not gifts we are born with. They are given to us by God when we **seek Him and desire to do His will**. We have been created to serve Him and these two attributes are His gifts to the person who seeks to do the Father's will with all his heart. Christ is formed in us when we seek Him and when we have fellowship with Him, He imparts His mind to us which includes spiritual wisdom and insight.

I have often used the example of Samson and Joseph, two men powerfully called by God. Both had purpose and destiny, both men's **families and nation** depended on their spiritual wisdom and insight. The major differences between these two men were Joseph's character and Samson's lack of character. A person of good character is a person with integrity and pure moral values. This person is **dependable and trustworthy**. Character reveals the heart of a person and unless truth forms the foundation of his life there can be no fellowship or communion with the Father. Both Samson and Joseph were endowed with power from on high. Both had a unique calling and destiny and both were defined by the depth or shallowness of their character.

Samson knew he had a major role to play in the future of Israel. His parents had been visited by the Angel of the Lord and Samson's destiny was spelled out by the Lord. Samson grew up knowing that the Philistines were the enemy, but he disregarded the Word of the Lord as well as the counsel of his parents and mingled with the Philistine women. He abused the gift of power and might that God had given him by using it for personal gain and revenge. Morally he grieved the Lord and his parents, by visiting prostitutes and finally the infamous Delilah was his downfall. It was only in the final moments of his life that Samson fulfilled the call of God on his life when he literally brought the house down on all the Philistine leaders. It took a serious time of introspection and suffering in the prison of the enemy to bring him to his senses. His eyes had been gouged out and he was chained up and forced to grind grain like a donkey. How different it could have been if Samson had only served the Lord, he would never have ended up enslaved by the enemy but instead enslaving the enemy. It is no different today. There are so many men and women, young and old who have chosen a life of sin and enslavement, when God has offered them a life of freedom and spiritual fulfilment.

Joseph was just such an exemplary man. From the beginning he chose to serve the Lord. We don't see much wisdom in the beginning of his young life when he boasted about his dreams, in fact it got him into a whole lot of trouble. God right on the other hand was there allowing Joseph to make his mistakes, but was manoeuvring destiny so that Israel as a Nation could grow from strength to strength in Egypt in a time of severe drought and hardship. Joseph had to learn to acquire wisdom and with time God started to multiply both wisdom and insight in his life. Wherever he found himself, God's favour and wisdom were recognised in him by those around him, causing him to rise up to the highest levels of promotion even to becoming prime minister of Egypt. Joseph's **strong moral character** formed the foundation of his success and caused him to walk in integrity no matter what the cost. Potiphar's evil wife could not even distract him with her sexual advances.

Against all odds, God's favour will cause doors to be opened that would appear impossible. God's favour (which I call uncommon favour because it goes beyond natural, human understanding) will take us beyond our wildest dreams when we hold onto God and the promises in His Word. The key to this uncommon favour is found in our daily relationship with the Father. God desires a relationship with us and He has put this very same desire in our hearts. When we respond to this, we start thinking His thoughts and His wisdom and insight starts flowing through us.

Establishing a Character Based on God's Wisdom

In today's spiritual exercise, meditate on the four different heart conditions in *Mark 4:15-20*. Which of the four would you categorize yourself? Maybe there are even two that you find overlapping in your life.

- The **hardened heart** shuts out the Word and the devil is there to snatch the seed of God's Word away.

- The seed on the gravel cannot take root and this indicates a **shallow and weak character**.

- Weeds in a person's life represent **worries and stress that overwhelm and strangle** the Word before it can take root.

- The good earth is the Christ-follower who **hears, understands, embraces and finally produces** a harvest beyond his wildest dreams.

Fertile hearts will embrace God's Word. With the help and strength of the Holy Spirit you can build a strong character and produce much fruit. With our God, ALL THINGS ARE POSSIBLE.

Day 7
Spiritual Disciplines

1 Corinthians 6:19-20 [NLT] Don't you realize that your body is the temple of the Holy Spirit, who lives in you and was given to you by God? You do not belong to yourself, for God bought you with a high price. So you must honour God with your body.

When we look at the universe, the order and discipline of all creation, we realise that we serve a God of order and discipline. Take a moment and imagine a universe without discipline. Planets would be hurtling out of control and our world would be in grave danger. Every tree and plant has pattern and order. Animals in their natural state have predictable habits and behaviour. The sun and moon rise and set everyday and the sea knows its boundaries. The only undisciplined creation is fallen man and fallen angels. God gave man a free will with which to serve and love Him, but instead man sold out to Satan and became as undisciplined and unruly as he.

Many people rebel against any form of discipline, except those who have found the true value and benefit thereof. **Discipline goes against the nature and character of fallen, sinful man.** Discipline speaks of order, restraint, control, and authority. Unless we are on the giving end we do not want to have a whole lot to do with it. A famous cliché, 'no pain, no gain' gives us insight into the benefits of living a disciplined life. All you have to do for a moment is stop to consider the outcome, the gain, and the long term benefits of surrendering to God's disciplines for your life. Believe it or not, there is FAR MORE to be gained from living by God's disciplines than living without them. God gives us enough grace to walk in His disciplines. His grace is the only saving factor that empowers us to perform the necessary disciplines required for a healthy godly lifestyle.

John 1:16 [AMP] For out of His fullness (abundance) we have all received [all had a share and we were all supplied with] one grace after another and spiritual blessing upon spiritual blessing and even favour upon favour and gift [heaped] upon gift.

When we come to the realisation that our bodies no longer belong to us, in fact they never have belonged to us, we will want God's precious disciplines in our lives. Before salvation our bodies were held captive by the god of this world, Satan, who was our step-father *[John 8:44]*. Through salvation our spirits were re-united with the Heavenly Father and we now have the freedom to worship and serve Him with our spirit, soul and body.

A disciplined life **releases the all-encompassing blessings** of God upon our lives. God's blessings will surround us and provide us with everything we need to achieve success and breakthrough. Jesus purchased our freedom, enabling us to stand before the Father without reproach and accusation. This is called grace, God's undeserved favour. We will not find the meaning of true godly grace in any dictionary; in fact it bears no resemblance to the worldly meaning of grace. When the Apostle Paul said that God's grace was sufficient for him, he knew that he would be able to overcome any and every obstacle that the devil could put in His way. God's grace (G-God's, R-Riches, A-At, C-Christ's, E-Expense) would cover everything he was ever going to need while he lived a disciplined life, focussed and dedicated to the Father. In *1 Corinthians 9:27* *[NLT]* Paul says *I discipline my body like an athlete, training it to do what it should. Otherwise, I fear that after preaching to others I myself might be disqualified.*

Understanding the Human Malady

I need to explain the difficulty many new believers often find themselves in. All their lives they may have been living or taught a certain way which to many may not appear wrong, performing acts and deeds that God in His Word considers sinful and even abominable. To give an example, the Word explicitly refers to sex as part of the marriage covenant and therefore living together without the commitment of marriage would be wrong in the eyes of God. Now the wonderful thing about conviction, if acted on, causes us to **obey the voice** of the Holy Spirit **who is living on the inside of us.** This **conviction** leads to a desire to **correct** the wrong. The opposite of conviction is condemnation and I can only ascribe this as a heaviness of spirit or a sense of guilt and hopelessness. This is usually brought about by disobedience to the voice of the Spirit and yielding to the voice of the devil. Satan steps in with judgement and accusation *[Revelation 12:10]*. The Word clearly tells us that our bodies are temples of the Holy Spirit and for that reason we need to incorporate the necessary disciplines that will bring our flesh and carnal desires under control *[1 Corinthians 6:19]*. Through knowledge of the Word we are able to change our way of thinking that will result in a new way of living. This is spiritual transformation in action.

Discipline is a way of conduct purposely implemented to achieve a desired goal, in this case, God's desired goal for our lives. To give an example, an Olympic athlete has to have a **disciplined training programme** in order to compete and hopefully win the coveted gold medal. It is no different when viewing our situation. We also have a goal which is far greater than winning a gold medal; it is finding the course and finishing the race of life that God predestined for us here on earth. Our race began when we were born. At birth we started an **eternal journey** that will ultimately culminate in heaven, living with the Father forever or hell, eternally separated from the father. Everything we do on this earth should be a **preparation for our eternal destination**. Can you for a moment imagine the terrible disappointment we will have when we meet the Father face-to-face and He reveals what His intended purpose and destiny for us was, but we failed to respond to His call.

Finding the Highest Attainable Goal

The only way that we can experience fulfilment on this earth is when we have set the Kingdom of God as our **highest attainable goal**. Only then will the rest of life on earth make sense and fall into place. Yes we must work, we must earn a salary and make money, we must provide for our families, but we must not allow things to dominate our lifestyles to the exclusion and neglect of the Kingdom of God.

For true transformation to take place in the spirit of man, **spiritual disciplines** must be incorporated into a life. We are living in a very undisciplined and out of control social environment and this is why the wheels of society are coming off. Biblical values are ridiculed, called old fashioned and considered an affront to human rights. Education systems have gone awry teaching innocent children wrong values and overstepping parental boundaries. God and the Bible have been banned from most school systems of the world especially countries that once based their constitutions on Biblical values. Whenever I see man resisting the disciplines of God I am reminded of an ant, commanding an elephant not to stomp on him. This ridiculous picture portrays fallen man waving his arms at heaven and saying "there is no God" or "God's Word is old fashioned and irrelevant".

Uncomfortable Restraint

The flesh of fallen man has rebelled against godly disciplines for six thousand years and can only be quelled by a deep, sincere and heart-felt change. The sin nature regards Biblical disciplines as an **uncomfortable restraint** and restrictive to the self-indulgent nature of the flesh. Only by resisting the urges and desires of the flesh with the help of the Holy Spirit, can the spiritual man have any **lasting breakthrough**. Without the necessary disciplines no one can draw close to God or even enter His presence.

Jesus, in many of his illustrations used nature and animals to emphasise a point. I want to use the illustration of the horse for it is probably one of the most magnificent creatures that the Lord created. It is of no use or value to mankind except it is trained and disciplined. In its wild state, its strength and beauty can only be observed but never touched or harnessed. Well we are very similar in our purpose here on earth. When we receive salvation we are in a wild and undisciplined state. Many choose to change, but many continue to live their old undisciplined ways. By not yielding to change we not only hurt ourselves, but we hurt others around us as well. For us to reach our full potential on this earth we have to allow the Holy Spirit to take control of the 'reins' of our lives and allow Jesus to 'reign' in our lives. His reign will steer us along the paths of wisdom, knowledge and revelation. By failing to do this we will remain wild, untrained, undisciplined and unusable, no good to ourselves, others or the Father. We will be unusable 'clay pots'.

Choose Life - Obey the Lord

Deuteronomy 30:19-20 [NLT] Today I have given you the **choice between life and death**, *between blessings and curses. Now I call on heaven and earth to witness the choice you make. Oh, that you would choose life, so that you and your descendants might live! You can make this choice by loving the Lord your God,* **obeying Him, and committing yourself firmly** *to Him. This is the key to your life. And if you love and obey the Lord, you will live long in the land the Lord swore to give your ancestors Abraham, Isaac, and Jacob.*

Some people **choose to live** life to the full, while others barely survive. Which category do you find yourself in?

Godly disciplines will enhance and enrich your Christian life and experience. God has placed in every life the desire to be an achiever; by incorporating godly disciplines in our day-to-day lives we will reach the highest, most fulfilling goals in our lives.

Godly wisdom will bring about the **dividing line**, or watershed in a Christian's life. The decisions we make in life determine the success or failure of our ventures and the quality of our lives.

What choices and what changes can you make in your day-to-day living that will enhance and change your mundane, ordinary existence? Every day with Jesus can be the most exciting and adventurous journey you have ever been on.

Week 2

Preparing the Soul of Man

Week 2
Preparing the Soul of Man

*James 1:21 [NLT] So get rid of all the filth and evil in your lives, and humbly accept the word God has planted in your hearts, for it has the **power to save your souls**.*

*Romans 12:2 [NKJV] And do not be conformed to this world, but be **transformed by the renewing of your mind**, that you may prove what is that good and acceptable and perfect will of God.*

The soul, unlike our spirit, is not directly connected to the Spirit of God and finds itself in a **place of constant conflict**. The soul consists of the intellect, will and emotions and that is why the **mind** is often called the battleground of man. The soul is torn between serving the Lord and following the wants and cravings of the flesh. In *Deuteronomy 6:5* the Father said we must love Him with all our heart (spirit), soul (mind) and body (flesh). Loving God also denotes serving Him - love is not just lip service, love must always flow into actions. Throughout the Psalms, David alternated between the heart and the soul of man. He had a profound revelation of worship and he found the key to subduing the carnal tendencies of the soul by worshipping **with** his soul. Although he lived under the law, his heart was so tuned into God and his love for God was reflected in words, deeds and actions. Now we know he slipped up many times, but his victory lay in his acknowledgement and repentance of sin. If David who lived in Old Testament times could walk in this revelation, how much more should we not be mastering the art of fellowship and intimacy with the Father? It is only through constant fellowship and relationship that we will succeed in our spiritual walk with the Lord.

The whole action of serving and worshipping the Father with our soul and body involves a very **high and consistent** degree of discipline. This is not cultivated overnight. When you plant a seed, there is a germination period. Germination requires a watering period (reading the Word and praying) and before long a little shoot appears and finally it starts resembling a tree. Within a few years it is bearing fruit, providing shade and shelter for birds and is beautiful to behold. All can eat of its fruit, be protected from heat and storms and the tree becomes a testimonial of godliness and beauty.

Our spirits have received salvation, but our souls (minds) have to be renewed through reading and meditating on the Word of God.

Here are some verses from the Psalms that will inspire you and prepare your soul to worship and serve the Lord:

Psalm 19:7 [NKJV] *The law of the Lord is perfect, converting the soul.*

Psalm 23:3 [NKJV] *He restores my soul; He leads me in the paths of righteousness For His name's sake.*

Psalm 25:20-21 [NKJV] *Keep my soul, and deliver me; Let me not be ashamed, for I put my trust in You. Let integrity and uprightness preserve me, for I wait for You.*

Psalm 42:1-2 [NKJV] *As the deer pants for the water brooks, So pants my soul for You, O God. My soul thirsts for God, for the living God. When shall I come and appear before God?*

Psalm 57:1 [NKJV] *Be merciful to me, O God, be merciful to me! For my soul trusts in You.*

Psalm 62:1-2 *[NKJV] Truly my soul silently waits for God; From Him comes my salvation. He only is my rock and my salvation; He is my defence; I shall not be greatly moved.*

Psalm 69:10 *[NKJV] When I wept and chastened my soul with fasting.*

Psalm 94:19 *[NKJV] In the multitude of my anxieties within me, Your comforts delight my soul.*

Psalm 107:9 *[NKJV] For He satisfies the longing soul, And fills the hungry soul with goodness.*

Psalm 116:7-8 *[NKJV] Return to your rest, O my soul, For the Lord has dealt bountifully with you. For You have delivered my soul from death, My eyes from tears, And my feet from falling.*

Psalm 119:28 *[NKJV] My soul melts from heaviness; Strengthen me according to Your word.*

Psalm 119:175 *[NKJV] Let my soul live, and it shall praise You; And let Your judgments help me.*

Psalm 120:2 *[NKJV] Deliver my soul, O Lord, from lying lips And from a deceitful tongue.*

Psalm 138:3 *[NKJV] In the day when I cried out, You answered me, And made me bold with strength in my soul.*

Psalm 142:7 *[NKJV] Bring my soul out of prison, That I may praise Your name; The righteous shall surround me, For You shall deal bountifully with me.*

Day 8
True Liberation of the Soul

---

*Matthew 11:29-30 [AMP] Take My yoke upon you and **learn** of Me, for I am gentle (meek) and humble (lowly) in heart, and **you will find rest** (relief and ease and refreshment and recreation and blessed quiet) for your souls. For My yoke is **wholesome** (useful, good — not harsh, hard, sharp, or pressing, but comfortable, gracious, and pleasant), and My burden is light and easy to be borne.*

True liberation must first be found in the spirit, before it can manifest in the soul of man. Mankind is always seeking ways to liberate the soul, but neglects to realise (through lack of knowledge) that the spiritual man is directly linked to its Creator. It is therefore only in HIM that we find true liberty. Through the rebirth of the spiritual man, we come to terms with who God is and where we fit into His overall plan. Only then will we find peace within ourselves *[Colossians 3:15]*. For us to have the **peace of God** ruling in our hearts and souls, we have to have **peace with God**. This is where 'soul therapy' begins. Our minds have been out of control like a ship without an anchor bobbing around on the vast ocean of life, grappling with issues and never finding lasting peace and stability. Jesus comes on the scene and offers us a haven of safety and protection in the form of a yoke. This is not a yoke of bondage or oppression; we've had enough of that all our lives, but a yoke of security and peace. Yoked with Jesus we will find a place of rest for our soul (mind) and a wonderful sense of relief that we are no longer carrying the burdens of life alone.

Man was never created to be alone, but after the fall in the Garden of Eden, his 'link' to God was severed. Jesus came and restored the 'missing link' and with the help of the Holy Spirit, He now reveals a process of change which removes the hindering factors that caused the breakdown in the first place. The will of man to disobey God is still present and must therefore be **surrendered daily** to the Lord. The way we surrender our will is by receiving Jesus' yoke and allowing the Holy Spirit on the inside of us to guide us back into fellowship with the Father.

This yoke is not a visible yoke, but the evidence or lack thereof can be seen in our actions of obedience and surrender to the Father's will. The yoke that Jesus offers is a **voluntary symbol** of our surrender and submission to Christ's Lordship. The true meaning and revelation of this yoke can only be revealed through a living, loving and daily relationship with the Father.

A Life of Consequences

We live lives of consequences. Most things that happen to us are a result of the **choices** we've made. **To not accept Christ's yoke** is to accept a life of unbearable burdens, unresolved problems and by Kingdom standards, an **'abnormal' lifestyle**. For illustration, in the use of the word 'normal' as opposed to 'abnormal', I place Jesus Christ at one end of the pendulum and the devil on the other end. When we received Jesus as our Saviour, we moved in the spirit from Satan's side of the pendulum to Jesus' side. In the spirit realm we moved from the kingdom of darkness into the Kingdom of God and absolute light *[Colossians 1:13]*. We were **spiritually delivered** from an abnormal, perverted kingdom into the perfect, sinless Kingdom. This transition heralded the beginning of our new life with Christ.

As we strive to change our behaviour and become more Christ-like we move towards 'normality', resembling the most normal and balanced man that ever walked the earth, Jesus Christ. The only way to measure the new nature is against the backdrop of the old. It would be scripturally sound to say that our old character resembled that of the god of this world, the devil, to whom we were enslaved *[John 8:44]*. True salvation reflects the **deep desires of the indwelling Holy Spirit** as we allow the Lord to live His life **in and through us**. Our words and deeds must reflect our love and service to our Saviour. The old selfish, self-centred nature is replaced by the new sacrificial and giving nature of the Holy Spirit. In simple language a truly born-again person radiates the love and character of Jesus.

Aside from the Christian faith, no ideology or religion can offer a person true and lasting spiritual freedom. But the problem with the symbol of the yoke is that people negatively associate it with restraint and a 'kill-joy' scenario. By not grasping the true meaning of the yoke of Christ, many Christians have remained stagnant and even regressed in their Christian commitment, never becoming true Christ-followers and disciples. **No person can be a true disciple of the Lord Jesus Christ without taking on the yoke of Christ**. I came out of the world system, in fact I was very much part of it. I was a radio broadcaster for seventeen years of my life. I was part of the music and entertainment industry and yet I was miserable and unfulfilled. I knew that life was more than what I was experiencing. At first when I was faced with the message of the cross and taking on the yoke of Christ's Lordship, it was a very daunting decision, for I had known no other life except the one I was living. I came to the realisation that there was more to life than I was experiencing and this drove me to take the **huge leap of faith**.

A New World

If I had known then what I know now, I would probably have served the Lord from a very young age. I have often felt that my life before Christ was such a waste, yet I learnt that all of life irrespective of time or age is a **preparation for the destiny** to which we are all born. The only difference is that not everyone takes the leap of faith into the new and unknown world of the Holy Spirit. Do not fear the spiritual dimension, but come to grips with the fact that we are first and foremost spiritual beings. Our mortal bodies will die and be raised as immortal bodies on 'resurrection day', and our spirits will live forever, hopefully with the Lord. The Father created our 'spirit being' and His original intention was to have fellowship with us and impart the secrets of His Kingdom to us, His special creation *[Psalm 8]*. Although He gave us our own identity and character, His ultimate intention was that we would love and serve Him with all our spirit, soul and body. For centuries He had to stand by and watch Satan deceive the children of this world. The Father gave us a free will and therefore could not interject or override our will, but He had a plan and **we were part of that redemption plan**.

There is a subtle **mystery surrounding the human will**. We do have a free will, but at the same time we would be fools to choose anything other than life. The Bible clearly states that we have to choose between life and death *[Deuteronomy 30:19]*. Not much of a choice when viewed from the Biblical point of view. So we either choose to serve the Lord and live a life under His protection and guidance, or we indirectly choose to be controlled by the devil serving him in his lusts and perverted ways. Demons seek a body through which they can operate and perform their devilish actions. The children of this world system are puppets and Satan and his demons are the puppeteers. We are in actual fact yoked either way. When we choose against the yoke of Christ, we take on the yoke of Satan whether we like it or not. His yoke is a yoke of tyranny in which we remain enslaved to sin. In contrast Jesus' yoke offers us true freedom and peace that can only come from the Son of God *[John 8:34]*.

In *Ephesians 6:12* we read of the spiritual battle and the operation of Satan and his cohorts. This scripture tells us that we are surrounded by spiritual beings but we need to know that all are not evil. On the contrary the Lord and His heavenly hosts **far outnumber the evil hordes** and they are just as hard at work fighting for us who have received salvation and call on the name of the Lord.

Hebrews 1:14 [AMP] Are not the angels all ministering spirits (servants) sent out in the service [of God for the assistance] of those who are to inherit salvation?

True Freedom is only Found in Christ's Yoke

Disciplines although constrictive, actually liberate our souls. We are not free to do as others do, but free to do what others cannot do. There is power in the disciplines of the yoke.

We are free agents, free from the bondage and chains of Satan. Being yoked with Jesus does not mean we are not free to do as we like, but free to do as we ought.

Who are You Yoked With?

- Jesus' invitation is to actually **exchange yokes**. We have the choice to be yoked with Satan to this world and live a life of bondage and oppression or be yoked with Jesus under His rule. He will teach you and show you that His burdens are light and easy to bear and you will even find rest in the midst of it all.

- Carefully consider the yoke in the light of today's opening scripture. You will come to the realisation that if you are going to walk in godly peace and wisdom, you actually **don't have a choice** but to accept Jesus' invitation.

- Are you ready to bring those burdens to the foot of the cross and come in under the yoke of Jesus? He said that He will help us lighten the load and make life and all its difficulties **easy to bear**. Just remember it is a **leap of faith** and without faith we cannot please the Lord *[Hebrews 11:6]*.

Day 9
Spiritual Power
Versus Soul Power

Matthew 16:24-26 [Kenneth S. Wuest] Then Jesus said to His disciples, If anyone is desiring to come after me, let him forget self and lose sight of his own interests, and let him pick up his cross and carry it, and let him be taking the same road with me that I travel, for whoever is desiring to save his soul-life shall ruin it, but whoever will pass a sentence of death upon his soul-life for my sake, shall find it. For what will a man be profited if he gain the whole world but forfeit his soul-life? Or, what shall a man give as an exchange for his soul-life?

Our journey today uncovers the dimension of the **soul-life** and Jesus' remedy for overcoming its **destructive influence on our eternal destiny.** Kenneth S. Wuest and the Amplified version have a very descriptive take on the actual Greek interpretation of the temporal (now) life and eternal life. **Firstly**, if we try to save our soul-life by holding onto the comforts and security of this temporal life, we will ruin our chances of eternity with the Father. **Secondly**, we are instructed to place a death sentence on our soul-life by walking away from the comforts and security of this world for Jesus' sake and then we will find eternal life. **Thirdly**, what could it possibly profit us to gain the whole world (all the stuff of this world) by giving ourselves to this soul-life, yet lose the Kingdom-of-God-life forever? **Fourthly**, what achievements and promises could this earthly, soul-life possibly offer us, even cause us to hang on to, in exchange for the Kingdom of God and

His innumerable and immeasurable promises?

In these four points we realise that Jesus is warning us to not love this world and its things **more than God**. I am sure you will not disagree with me if I say that the Father knows us and our 'loves' a whole lot better than we know ourselves. People will vehemently deny that they are attached to this life and the things of this life, but when put to the test, most are sure to fail dismally.

One thing we can be assured of is that **we will be tested**, because there is a war going on for our souls and the Father wants us body, soul and spirit, not just our reborn spirits. We are deceived if we think that we can serve God with our spirits and allow our body and soul to do what they like. In my years of serving the Lord I have learnt that there are no half measures with the Father. It is all or nothing.

Discerning the Difference

My wife and I were in conversation, debating the aspect of the soul-driven church as opposed to the Spirit-driven church. The church in this context is not a building or an organization, but a body of believers led, trained and taught by what is called the five-fold ministry *[Ephesians 4:11-12]*. This was a very challenging discussion because I realised that we are walking on very thin ice and if we do not **discern the difference** between the soulish and the spiritual, we could deceive the flock of God. Sunday gatherings and home fellowship meetings should never just be feel-good experiences. I could preach good motivational messages, never challenging believers to change their lifestyles and all I'll have done is created a 'soul-powered', self-centred, self-absorbed 'religion'. As a shepherd of God's flock I have a tremendous responsibility to point the way and give direction, keeping the congregation on the straight and narrow path. My personal goal is to help believers become more Christ-like and find their destiny and purpose in life.

*Matthew 7:13-14 [AMP] Enter through the narrow gate; for wide is the gate and spacious and broad is the way that **leads away to destruction**, and many are those who are entering through it. But the gate is narrow (**contracted by pressure**) and the way is straitened and compressed that leads away to life, and few are those who find it.*

In this scripture we see the danger of being drawn to the broad and spacious highway which many will choose because it offers false comfort, easy access and a compromised lifestyle. The narrow way on the other hand is **constrictive to the soul of man**, and often appears to squash the 'fun' out of the soul-life of a person. The soul and flesh will always want to break away and will even pervert scripture to do so. Think of the wrong lifestyles people are living, where sex outside of marriage and sexual perversions have become the acceptable norm. The Word is twisted to suit unscriptural lifestyles and GRACE has been misinterpreted as an excuse for 'alternative living'. God is reduced to our human level of thinking and phrases like, "God is love and He understands the nature of man for after all He made us like this" etc. are commonly heard. This kind of reasoning stifles the spirit of man, grieves the Spirit of God and keeps people on the broad and destructive highway ultimately leading to spiritual death. God loves us dearly and He desires us to return to that original pattern He created, not the devil's sick perverted pattern. In order for us to be re-united with the Father and live with Him eternally, He has released the power to bring healing, correction and the ability to overcome ALL of our soulish wrongdoing and thinking.

Overcoming Soul Power

The soul in the biblical context is the mind of man, the seat of our emotions, intellect and will. It is in the soul that we win or lose the battles of life depending on our commitment to God. We need to discern the wrong thinking processes in our minds. The soul, being the place of decision making, could be called the intelligence centre of the body, receiving and issuing commands to the rest of the body. For any change to come about, the mind (soul) has to be reprogrammed through consistent intake of the Word of God. This is the first and most important discipline right alongside prayer and communion with the Father.

I believe that a lack of spiritual perception and understanding causes people to underestimate the power of the Holy Spirit and therefore they place their trust in the power of the soul dimension. If we are what we think, then our thinking needs to line up with God's thinking. It's this very thinking process that got us into trouble in the first place. Just ask Adam and Eve, they will tell you. God puts no value or faith in the soul (mind) of man, that's why He made available to us the Mind of Christ *[Philippians 2:5]*. When we tune our spirits to hear from God, the Holy Spirit reveals the Mind of Christ to us and we are able to think like Him and act like Him. We will find ourselves rejecting wrong thinking processes and replacing them with godly thoughts. This will impact our lifestyles and we will discover that a slow but sure transformation is taking place as we come in line with God's Word.

Establishing a Godly Mindset

- What wrong thought processes do you need to address that you know are **hindering** you from entering into the fullness of God's Kingdom.

- By memorising scriptures we train our minds to think new thoughts. The Word of God brings **light and life** to our mind and soul dimension and illuminates the wrong thinking processes.

- Remain sensitive to the voice of the Holy Spirit on the inside and allow Him to **guide your thinking**. A prayer I love to pray is: "Lord let your thoughts become my thoughts and let Your will become my will".

- You will not change overnight, but this one thing I can promise you, if you persist YOU WILL CHANGE and you will find everything around you changing as well. Become a God-pleaser not a man-pleaser and you will influence others to do the same.

Day 10
A Soul Transformation

Romans 12:1-2 [NLT] *Don't copy the behaviour and customs of this world, but let God transform you into a new person by **changing the way you think**. Then you will learn to know God's will for you, which is good and pleasing and perfect.*

James 1:21 [NLT] *So get rid of all the filth and evil in your lives, and humbly accept the word God has planted in your hearts, for it has the **power to save your souls**.*

Transformation of the soul speaks of a conversion or make-over of the mind. This transformation can **only** be possible by **integrating various spiritual disciplines** into a life. Before transformation, the soul of a person is a very **undisciplined and unsupervised** entity. The mind and the will of a person has been unbridled without God, doing its own thing, living without boundaries and in most cases oblivious of its Creator. We have been wonderfully made *[Psalm 139]* but without spiritual disciplines, the soul and body remain uncontrolled and undisciplined.

Daily we are bombarded through the media with the whole idea of physical make-overs. Aside from costing a small fortune, much emphasis is placed on the fact that it can and will 'transform' a life, bring happiness and even fulfilment. But nothing on the 'label' says that it is short-lived and temporary. We can improve our appearance all we like and even come out looking like super-stars, but if we don't transform our soul, there can be no lasting or satisfying change. Joy, peace and contentment are the outward manifestation of the inner state of a person. It cannot be bought; nothing on this earth can produce it, and the only person who can give it is our Heavenly Father.

Bearing His Image and Likeness

Genesis 1:26-27 [AMP] God said, Let Us [Father, Son, and Holy Spirit] make mankind in Our image, after Our likeness, and let them have complete authority over the fish of the sea, the birds of the air, the [tame] beasts, and over all of the earth, and over everything that creeps upon the earth. So God created man in His own image, in the image and likeness of God He created him; male and female He created them.

The Father made us to reflect Him and bear His identity and character. He wanted us to think like Him, look like Him and act like Him. If you meditate for a moment on this, you would probably agree that we fall far short of God's original intention. We resemble Him in our physical appearance, Jesus showed us that, but our character and soul are far removed from that original design. This does not mean He wanted us to be puppets for then He would have made us identical. He gave us each our own personalities, with our different unique appearances but in our basic needs, character, soul and values, He wanted us to resemble Him.

'But God'! I love this phrase because it speaks of an intervention that we are incapable of achieving in our own strength. In short, a supernatural intervention was wrought through the working of the Holy Spirit within us. In our daily scripture reading we make two observations:

1. We can **change the way we think**.

2. We can **transform our souls** (minds) through the power that is released to us as we take in and apply God's Word in our lives.

We come to the conclusion that the Lord does not accept our way of thinking; in fact He regards it as filth and evil. Through our act of voluntary surrender, the Holy Spirit empowers us and gives us the ability to change our thinking processes.

Many years ago we had a student who was virtually illiterate. He battled to read and write and he had never progressed beyond grade six. He was so desperate to do the Bible College that we agreed to give him oral examinations because of his literacy problems. Well, we were all in for a 'God surprise' as the entrance of God's Word gave light and understanding to his mind. We saw *Psalm 119:130* in action. When came examination time, he was able to partake in the examinations with the other students. His reading of the Word improved dramatically. It sometimes requires desperate measures to achieve goals, and this student knew that with the power of God he was going to achieve his goal. It changed his entire outlook and quality of life.

The question is: ARE YOU READY AND WILLING TO CHANGE? This change will affect every area of your life. You will start doing things differently because you will be thinking differently. Your behaviour will change and this will have an effect on your social life, but most importantly you will feel different because your soul will be in a process of transformation. The entrance of God's Word brings light and understanding to your mind and the peace of God will flood your soul.

Peace of Mind and Soul

Philippians 4:7 *[AMP] And God's peace [shall be yours, that **tranquil state of a soul assured** of its salvation through Christ, and so fearing nothing from God and being content* *with its earthly lot of whatever sort that is, that peace] which transcends all understanding shall garrison and mount guard over your hearts and minds in Christ Jesus.*

This scripture in the Amplified Bible highlights the state of a soul that has made the right choices or should I say 'God choices' and finds himself in a good place spiritually, emotionally and physically. God's power is released through His Word. When we hold onto His promises by faith, we are able to overcome and bring about deliverance in the soul and eventually the flesh dimension.

Good Intentions Will Not Save the Soul

Unless definite disciplines like prayer and reading of the Word are incorporated in our lives, **there can be no change**. We can have all the good intentions in the world, but we need the power of prayer and the Holy Spirit to bring our good intentions to light. The Message Bible in *Matthew 26:41* warns us of the weakness of the soul; *Stay alert; be in prayer so you don't wander into temptation without even knowing you're in danger. There is a part of you that is eager, ready for anything in God. But there's another part that's as lazy as an old dog sleeping by the fire.*

True Christ followers do not have problems with their souls, they are spiritually alive to God and dead to sin and its lures *[Romans 6:11]*. This state of 'deadness' is subject to change if the necessary disciplines are not adhered to. Many years ago, God brought a wonderful man of God across my path in the form of Dion Robert of the Ivory Coast. Brother Dion's forthright approach to sinful man and repentance was so refreshing and eye-opening. He made the statement that he only works with 'dead' people. The 'living' ones give him too much trouble. I realised that for too long we in the West had been nurturing and pampering the soul of man, instead of dealing with it definitively and decisively. Only then can we move into the spiritual power and authority of God's Word.

The Bible emphatically states that we were **delivered out of** the dominion of darkness into the Kingdom of God *[Colossians 1:13]*. This **changed our eternal destiny** but we still have to deal with our soul and flesh on a daily basis. We cannot reason that this only applied to our spirits and then think that all is 'dandy' if we continue in our old ways.

This deliverance is meant to be **body, soul and spirit**. Initially it is a spiritual deliverance but the Lord expects the transformation of our souls and bodies to come in line with the transformed state of our spirits. **God did for us what we could not do for ourselves.** He changed the state of our spiritual being but we have it in our power to change the soul and body with the help of His Holy Spirit now living inside of us.

If we do not change our behaviour we will find ourselves with one foot in the world and the other foot in the Kingdom. We will end up making soulish or carnal decisions and the repercussions will be very detrimental to our walk with the Lord.

Preparing the Soul For Transformation

- Many Christians may well be far down the road in their transformation process, but most Christians I know, including myself, still have a long way to go. What DISCIPLINES will you need to incorporate in your personal life that will **stop you from wandering off into temptation?**

- These 21 days are designed to take you to a new level in the spirit, but **the onus is on you** to change. Seriously analyse your commitment to change because without determination you will not be able to bring about any lasting change.

- Do not forget to incorporate prayer and the reading of God's Word in today's exercise, because without it, you will only have good intentions.

Day 11
An Instrument
of 'Soul' Deliverance

*Matthew 10:32 [Kenneth S. Wuest] And he who does not take his cross and **take the same road with Me** which I take, is not worthy of Me. He who has found his soul-life, shall ruin and render it useless, and he who has **passed a sentence of death upon his soul-life** for My sake shall find it.*

I always try to practically picture what Jesus was speaking about, because there was often interplay between the spiritual and the natural meaning. In this case Jesus was not speaking of physical death on a cross, but rather that we were to die to the lusts and wants of the soul and flesh and live for Him by serving Him with our spirit, soul and body. The disciples were not always happy with Jesus' comments for after all they believed He was 'The Deliverer' that would rescue Israel from the Roman oppression. The deliverance that Jesus referred to was not comfortable, to be honest it was very stressful to the soul and flesh of man. In fact His deliverance did very little to alleviate the Jewish plight in Israel. What they failed to realise however, was that Jesus' deliverance was the **ultimate liberation** that would free them, not just for the 'here and now', but for eternity. Many people find themselves in an immediate crisis situation where Jesus gets looked upon as the spare wheel of a car which is needed only during times of trouble. When the Lord does not meet their immediate need they become disillusioned and cynical.

The cross that Jesus referred to at the time was an instrument of death used by the Romans to enforce law and order in their captured colonies. They would hang criminals and law-breakers on crosses alongside the highways as examples to possible law-breakers and rebels, demonstrating the punishment they could expect if they incited rebellion or committed any crimes. In other words the cross was destined for all law-breakers. Seen in a spiritual context, the human race, since Adam and Eve, have never stopped breaking God's laws. Since the fall of mankind we have been unable to keep God's moral laws because of the sin nature we acquired when Adam and Eve chose to disobey God and heed the voice of Satan in the Garden of Eden.

The Father's Ultimate Plan

God gave man a free will even though He in His foreknowledge knew that man would make the wrong choice just as the devil did and was cast out of heaven [Isaiah 14:12]. God had given mankind His Spirit and His image, but also a free will with which to serve Him and have fellowship with Him. There is however an amazing factor involved: The Father wanted to put His creation through a process of refining as with fine gold. This process would deal with the spirit, soul and body of man. God wanted a Body of believers that would **choose unreservedly** to love Him and Him alone. It's a scary thought, but the Father knew that there was a **'heart condition'** in man that needed testing and changing. The Father wanted a total heart surrender and not partial or forced submission. Think of two people in love, neither person wants to settle for second best. Each party wants to know that their partner loves them unreservedly and that it will be a 'forever' commitment. Unfortunately because of the fickleness and sinful nature of man, the result is often failure and divorce, but the original intention was good and pure. God had a plan that would enable mankind to make the right decision and follow through with it forever. This decision involves a **choice** together with the **power** to transform. When we make the right choices in life, we can expect God to bless and empower our choices.

The Father's ultimate plan was to model the person that He desired for us to be and no one could do it better than He. **Jesus was that Model**, God's only Son who came to pave the way and show mankind how it could be accomplished. The only legal route that the Father could take was through sacrifice and blood. The life of man is in the blood, therefore there has to be a shedding of blood for life to be given and received *[Leviticus 17:11]*. The whole sacrificial system of the Old Testament was a picture of Jesus on the cross, the final sacrifice. The power that was needed to overcome the devil and his attack on God's creation was attained through the blood of Jesus. *Romans 5:9-10 [NLT] And since we have been made right in God's sight by the **blood of Christ**, He will certainly save us from God's condemnation. For since our friendship with God was **restored by the death of His Son** while we were still His enemies, we will certainly be saved through the life of His Son.*

We now have the power and ability together with the indwelling presence of Christ, to overcome the attacks against our soul and flesh. What was impossible before became possible **through the cross**. In the case of our soul, we can 'crucify' wrong and sinful thoughts and fantasies and replace them with good and godly principles and disciplines based on the Word of God. Satan cannot read our minds, so He can only gauge what we are thinking by our conduct. When we receive wrong thoughts, we should immediately replace them with good and godly thoughts and act accordingly.

This will displace Satan's seat in our soul. The body and its desires will eventually have to follow suit as we overcome Satan and his attacks against our minds.

Jesus came and modelled a lifestyle that was foreign to all. No man had ever demonstrated such a selfless, sacrificial, and surrendered mode of living as His. His lifestyle went against the grain of society with its selfish, self-centred existence. His motives were pure and untainted by evil desires and greed. He infuriated the religious community because He exposed their hypocrisy and pretentious religion. The poor loved Him because He emanated **love**, **hope** and **faith**.

A Criminal's Death

Jesus' final act of love was to take on the sins of the world. He who was no criminal, who never had a sin or blot against His name, was the Father's sinless Lamb. He became the sacrifice, suffered the death of a criminal so that we, who deserved a criminal's death, could have eternal life. He knew that He was destined for the cross, but He also knew that He was bringing salvation to the world. When He pointed to the cross, He was revealing a lifestyle that would please the Father and establish communication once again between mankind and its Creator. In the sinful condition that we were in, we could never achieve any form of acceptance from the Father. There was only one way and it was through the blood of Jesus.

The cross has two bars. On the horizontal bar arms are stretched out as a sign of total surrender, acknowledging our sin natures and also **acknowledging our inability to save ourselves**. The vertical bar reaches from heaven to earth and is a 'two-way receptor' connecting us to heaven and heaven to us. When we cry out to the Father, He sees Jesus' blood on that cross and looks down through the sacrifice (the veil of Christ's flesh) *[Hebrews 10:20]* and rescues us. We are forgiven, our sins are paid for and our eternal journey into God's Kingdom is paved by Jesus' everlasting sacrifice.

The Enemy's Ploy

The whole aspect of the cross is contrary to the instincts and values of society. Satan has brainwashed the world by focussing mankind on self. Humanism and human rights have replaced Christianity as the standard by which to live. This causes God's creation to ignore Him and focus on living selfish, self-centred lives, pampering the 'self' nature. The very idea of a selfless and sacrificial lifestyle is totally foreign and even offensive to the world. I hate to burst your bubble, but it just happens to be the language of the Kingdom of God and as such every Kingdom citizen **has no choice** if they are to finish the race and reach their eternal destination.

When we realise that we were **created by God for His purposes**, we will move into a whole new dimension of living. It will change the way we think, act and live *[2 Timothy 1:9]*.

It May Appear Difficult, But It's Not Impossible

This has been a very difficult chapter in our 21-day journey, but I pray that you will receive in your hearts the gravity of the message. Allow the Father to reveal to you what areas you need to bring to the cross and ask Him for the power to overcome. We serve an awesomely powerful and very loving Father.

- **Loving the Father is serving Him with our minds and our thoughts**. Loving is a demonstrative act of giving and yielding. We cannot say we love and not show it. Loving is far more than lip service. We are to love with our spirit, our soul and our body.

- So many people say they love their husbands or wives yet they are unfaithful in thought and deed. The same applies to our Heavenly Father. We cannot profess to love Him yet in our minds and flesh we commit sinful thoughts and acts. I have often heard the phrase 'talk is cheap', well the Father knows our thoughts and sees our actions.

Day 12

Tough Love to the 'Soulish' Ego

---

*John 12:24-26 [NLT] I tell you the truth, unless a kernel of wheat is planted in the soil and dies, it remains alone. But its death will produce many new kernels — a plentiful harvest of new lives. **Those who love their life in this world will lose it.** Those who care nothing for their life in this world will keep it for eternity. Anyone who wants to be my disciple must follow me, because my servants must be where I am. And the Father will honour anyone who serves me.*

The power of the ego must never be underestimated. The ego is totally integrated into the character and personality of man. There is a positive side to ego which we touch on when we have to counsel people on their lack of self-worth and self-esteem. People are often so run down and emotionally fragile that all they need to see is their value and worth through the eyes of Jesus. They are then well on their way to recovery. Notice I said 'through the eyes of Jesus'. Satan has brought out the sick perverted side of the ego, the side that needs to die and be buried. I will be focussing on its negative aspects and the adverse effect on the soul of man. The ego is most times responsible for keeping the soul dimension alive, which is offensive to the Lord. In one of the explanations in the Encarta Dictionary, 'ego' is defined as an inflated opinion of self, an exaggerated sense of self-importance and a feeling of superiority to other people. Most of us have experienced the downside of the ego and it **alienates** us from the Father because of the total focus on the self-centred nature. Until we have died to self and status, we won't see the manifestation of God's glory working in our lives. John the Baptist summed it up very clearly when he said "I must become less so that He (Jesus) can become greater" *[John 3:30]*. John, you must remember, was the main attraction at the time that Jesus entered into ministry. If John had allowed his ego to rule, he would have been offended by his cousin who was taking centre stage, causing John to fade off the scene. Instead we see a remarkable manifestation of humility and selflessness as John steps back and acknowledges that Jesus **IS** the only begotten Son of God. John knew that this was his purpose and mission in life, to point to the One who was also his Saviour. This should be the attitude of every born-again child of God. We have to die to self destructive egos and step into our earthly Kingdom purpose.

Why earthly Kingdom purpose? So many Christians separate the Kingdom of God and their daily activities. Unless we bring purpose and Kingdom rule into daily work and leisure (everything we say and do) we cannot serve God fully or have any lasting success in life.

A Fool's Heart

We are often afraid to appear foolish, but that is part of the 'tough love' process through which the ego must go. We are not to love our lives, we are to love God above ALL else and if being a fool will get the job done, then so be it. Many years ago, I chose to die to this world and what people said about me. It was not easy, in fact it was very difficult, and still is, that I had to apply 'tough love' to my soul and ego if I was going to receive God's wisdom and acceptance. The human being loves flattery and acceptance, which strokes the ego and pride of man. When we opt to follow the Lord and 'apply the cross' to our soul and intellect, it deals a deadly blow to our self-centredness. I heard a description of 'ego' that sums up the predicament of many who refuse to deal with pride and arrogance: **E-edging G-God O-out**. This is exactly what we do when we do not deal with wrong attitude.

New life can only come forth out of death and Jesus offered us everything pertaining to Kingdom life and victory through His death. The condition to receiving this new life means that we will have to give up this world and all the plans we have had and surrender to Jesus' world. This does not mean we lose our focus and vision and stop living, but we **re-focus** and God gives us a new vision where He plays an **integral part in all we do.** God re-adjusts our outlook and the amazing part is that this perception is often a lot bigger and much better than we ever envisaged for ourselves. The process that Jesus used as an example is that of a kernel of grain that has to be planted in the soil and die so that it can sprout and eventually bear fruit. We have to bury our egos in the soil of Christ's Kingdom and allow the process of death to take place so that we can be transformed into another form, totally usable and productive in the hands of our Heavenly Father. This process I call 'death of a personal vision' and 'birth of a God-vision'.

'Tough love' is a programme used to help parents and children re-establish broken down boundaries and disciplines with the purpose of bringing order and sanity back into a home. It is often a very traumatic programme for both the child and the parents. It deals toughly with rebellious and out-of-control relationships, establishing respect and love in a home again. Godly disciplines have to be imposed on the rebellious and lawless soul of a person. I have realised a long time ago that God loves us too much to leave us the way we are. Jesus knew the pain we would have to go through and sent His Holy Spirit to help us and empower us to succeed, leaving us with no excuse for failure. We have to be **desperately dissatisfied** with our spiritual condition before we will want to change.

The Death Sentence

Tough love means you will have to pass the death sentence daily with regards to your soul. This is a **discipline** that must never be overlooked. Every day you must take charge of your soul. The Kingdom of God and the dominion of darkness are two different 'planets'; just so with the spirit and soul, they are literally two different worlds living in one body. Have you ever entered a room, or been part of a conversation, or been in a meeting where you felt you were far removed from present company, in fact you literally felt like you were from another planet. Well, where do you think all the sci-fi movies got their ideas from? Satan knows that you are from another planet, the Kingdom of God 'planet' and that you think and act in a way that is contrary to this earthly, carnal, demonic 'planet'. Satan knows that as a Kingdom citizen, you can outwit him anytime with the help of the Holy Spirit. With the Mind of Christ we have full access to God's throne room; we think differently, we act differently. This transformation of the soul can only come about as we allow the Spirit of God to 'eclipse' our soul, bringing in light and expelling all darkness, obscuring and hiding us from this world and its evils. There are no shadows in God's light and His light will expose the shadows of sin in our lives.

The Lie Detector Test

If there is one aspect of life that can be **desperately deceitful**, then it is the ego. We often hide pride under a guise of false humility and pretention. In the Bible Jesus was watching the rich who gave alms to be seen and acknowledged, yet it was the widow's giving that got the Lord's attention. The Pharisees were constantly rapped over the knuckles because of their religious hypocrisies.

If you were subjected to a lie detector test and your ego was the topic of examination, in which areas do you honestly think you would fail?

Are you ready to **apply the death sentence** to the 'ego areas' that are offensive and harmful to your Christian walk and which alienate you from the Father's presence *[Romans 8:38-39]*?

Day 13
Soul Preparation in Action

*Galatians 4:19 [AMP] My little children, for whom I am again suffering birth pangs until Christ is completely and permanently **formed (moulded) within you**.*

When the Apostle Paul used the terminology of moulding he was referring to the soulish dimension that the church of Galatia had allowed itself to get into. He was agonising over their sad spiritual condition because of the deception that had crept in. The aspect I wish to highlight is that he was calling them back into a state of spiritual soundness by allowing the Lord to mould and form them into **a continuing state of completeness in Christ**. The Galatians did not realise that they had become a soul-driven or soul-powered Body of believers instead of being Spirit-driven and empowered. On the one hand they were practising legalism as a qualification for salvation and 'spiritual' acceptance while on the other there was the aspect of false liberty that was compromising the values and disciplines laid out in God's Word.

We often hear of people who cover their sin under the mantle of God's grace, not realising the serious danger to their spiritual walk. Grace is God's strength and power to help us overcome carnal, fleshly weaknesses, not to create loopholes to continue in the hope that the Lord will overlook our sin and compromise. I have challenged people on wrong lifestyles and have often been met with a very laid back attitude of: "Yes Pastor, that is all very well for you, but surely God does not expect us 'normal' folk to be like you". This just takes the wind out of my sails. The very purpose of my being here is to help, teach and admonish people to live just like I am trying to live, in patterning my life after Jesus Christ. I will stand before the judgement seat with everyone else and together we will answer for how we either failed or succeeded in submitting to the Word and Truth of the Bible.

There has to be a preparation of the soul where we literally have to force our will and mind to come in line with the Holy Spirit. Compromise can and will ultimately cost us our salvation. The doctrine of 'once saved always saved' is not scriptural. This would be a big incentive to continue in our old ways, and we would never have to change.

Aligning the Soul With the Spirit

Daily I find myself locked in a continuous spiritual battle, aligning the soul and flesh with my spirit which has been transformed. This process of alignment is going to take an **ongoing soul preparation** until **Christ is formed** in me. Our spirits are already saved and seated in heavenly places with Jesus *[Ephesians 2:6]*, but our agony is getting our souls and minds centred on heavenly things instead of being caught up with this world and all its nonsense *[Colossians 3:2]*. If we could only grasp the truth that in the world, everything we do must be done with the Kingdom-of-God mission in mind. If you are a teller in the bank, then be the best teller in the bank. Let your light shine, walk in integrity and be filled with His joy, so that people will stop and ask 'what's your recipe for life'. This is Kingdom living and the children of this world will be drawn to it.

The gap between the soul and the born-again spirit can be compared to the distance between the north and south poles; two extreme opposites. Our initial deliverance was a spiritual deliverance when the Spirit of Christ came to **live in**

us and gives us the certainty that we will be sharing His glory one day *[Colossians 1:27]*. This promise that Christ has given us is based on His assurance that you and **I will make it**, or Paul would not have made the statement. Our challenge however, is to align our souls with the Spirit of God and this will produce the hope of glory. When we are out of alignment and harbouring sin in our lives, we live in condemnation and can have no hope of glory or blessing.

The Great Potter

When my daughter Charmaine designed the cover for this book, it was so appropriately in line with the transformation theme. My wife shed some light on the art of pottery and it was quite a revelation, for I saw a picture of our Heavenly Father preparing us for eternity. As I take you through the process I want you to envisage God as the Potter and you as the clay. This is 'soul preparation' in action. The preparation process of clay is very important. A potter can only use a moist and pliable piece of clay just as our Heavenly Father can only speak to us through His Word and His Spirit. We have to be washed daily with the washing of the water of the Word *[Ephesians 5:26]*. God's Word keeps us pliable (moist) and flexible every day. Repentance and forgiveness are two very vital foundational disciplines in every child of God's life. By failing to walk in these two disciplines the soul gets hardened.

Once the potter has selected his piece of clay, he proceeds to knead and pound the clay removing all bubbles and hard particles that would cause cracking and damage during the firing process. If the clay is not properly prepared, once it has been baked in the kiln there is no turning back. The heat transforms the molecules in the clay and it can never return to it's original state. If the potter is satisfied that the clay is ready for the wheel, then the actual throwing and moulding process begins. Unlike the firing process there can be many trial runs. If it doesn't work the first time, the potter kneads and pounds the clay again and again until he turns out the perfect item. This process can be repeated many times and the clay can even be left for long periods under plastic wrappings in a moist condition until further use. We see God's grace in action when time and time again we fall and stumble, but every time we seek Him, He is there to pick us up and restore us back into fellowship with Him. Every time we stumble we cause our own pain, but when our Potter takes us in His warm and healing hands, we are restored to life and health.

The Father's Picture of You

The picture that the Father has of you and me was in His mind long before we were even born. He foresaw our struggles, therefore He shares in our hardships, He is preparing those who are willing to be vessels fit to contain His glory [Psalm 139] and this preparation is a soul preparation. The quality of our craftsmanship is not in our physical appearance or gifting because they are God's gifts to us, but **our quality is in the measure of surrendered usefulness** to the King and His Kingdom. God needs us to remove all the impurities and blockages in our soul so that we can radiate His glory. The Father will never share His glory with sinful flesh.

Take Time to Consider Your Soul-Condition

How many times will the Potter have to pound, knead and reshape you? Animals are often quicker to learn from negative experiences than we are. They adjust quicker to conditioning therapy. We have the 'in built' qualities of hope and faith but fail to see that it is many times misdirected. We have to re-align ourselves to match the picture God has for us in His mind.

- **Re-align your focus** and ask the Holy Spirit to give you the power and ability to overcome soulish issues that are seriously hampering your spiritual well-being.

- **Take your eyes off other people** and their shortcomings; do not use them as an excuse for sin. Every one of us individually has a responsibility to the Father to correct, to adjust and to re-align our lives to come in line with the Word of God.

- There is **no such thing as a half-truth or a half-measure**. This is compromise and you may as well go your own way and face the consequences.

- Write down every compromising aspect in your life today and ask the Father to forgive you. There is **tremendous power in forgiveness** and the freedom that comes with it goes beyond description.

Day 14

Transforming a Fearful Soul

*2 Timothy 1:7 [AMP] For God did not give us a spirit of timidity (of cowardice, of craven and cringing and fawning fear), but [He has given us a spirit] of power and of love and of **calm and well-balanced mind** and discipline and self-control.*

Fear is the absence of faith and without faith it is impossible to please the Father *[Hebrews 11:6]*. I want to take it a shocking step further. To fear is **to deny the presence of God** and secondly to deny that He can do a better job than you or I. Meditate on this point for a moment, because you may be angry and deny this fact by saying, "but I do believe in God". Well that may be so, but so do the demons and that did not stop them falling out of God's grace and favour *[James 2:19]*.

Fear is the **enemy of our soul**. Fear and fearful thoughts are construed in the mind and if not 'taken captive' and re-aligned with the Word of God can cause us to become unbalanced and out of control as we see in today's scripture.

A person does not battle with fear in the spirit, because our spirit is the dwelling place of the Holy Spirit and the Father said He has NOT given us a spirit of fear but of power, love and a sound mind. It is in our soul where Satan still has access through the senses and through our surroundings that we see and hear things that evokes the spirit of fear. We have lived for so long under the dictatorship of Satan who rules through fear and doubt that we have to re-adjust our 'soulish periscope'. A periscope is an instrument used in a submarine to detect possible dangers above the water. When a submarine is submerged under water, it cannot see dangers lurking on the surface of the sea, it is oblivious of impending harm. By hoisting a periscope above the water it views through various lenses and prisms the surface of the sea and can detect the enemy without the enemy knowing that he is being observed.

There is a wonderful analogy in the periscope, for we also have been given a 'spiritual periscope' through which we can see and observe the enemy. Jesus said that He would never leave nor forsake us, but that He would send us the Holy Spirit to live inside of us. The Holy Spirit would become our 'periscope' warning us, preparing us through the spirit of faith to discern the enemy and stand against his onslaughts.

Discern the Enemy of Your Soul

No good general goes to war without full knowledge of his enemy and the possible tactics that will be used against him. The general will gather as much information as possible and strategise the enemy's defeat. It is no different for the child of God. We have been given the full briefing of Satan's tactics in the Bible so we must never neglect to read the 'Manual'. Many have read it, but not believed in it because they never saw it through God's **Kingdom glasses of faith**. You can only **fight fear with faith**. It is as simple as that.

Fear is a **product of the soul** (mind) just as faith is the **product of the heart** (spirit). Fear was never part of the Father's impartation to us, but when Satan was cast away from the presence of God, he entered the world of darkness and fear. To be separated from God the Creator of all things is to be removed from life and faith and cast into a place of death and fear. Satan's dominion works in direct opposition to

God's Kingdom and he subtly uses principles and values of the Kingdom, twists and perverts them and throws them right back at us. The Message Bible comforts us in *1 Corinthians 10:13* by saying that *no test or temptation that comes your way is beyond the course of what others have had to face. All you need to remember is that God will never let you down;* **He'll never let you be pushed past your limit;** *He'll always be there to help you come through it.*

In this scripture we are told that Satan cannot use any tactics that are not **common to man**. In other words his tactics are common, they are ordinary and they are strategies that we ought to be familiar with. This really encourages me, because I know that my God is 'uncommon'. He lives in the dimension of the supernatural and He can do things far above and beyond anything you and I can possibly even imagine. The big dilemma that we face is **lack of knowledge** and a realisation of who and how big our God is. If I have knowledge of the devil and his plans and I have knowledge of God and His mighty power and ability, I have power to overcome. **Knowledge of God's Word is power**.

Instilling Faith Disciplines

The unrenewed mind (soul) can often be compared to a runaway train on the verge of being derailed. Unless some form of breaking is applied, the train will be in serious trouble. When a mind is unrestrained, spiritual growth is suppressed. To overcome the issues of the soul and stop it getting us into trouble, we have to **sow time and energy into spiritual activities and disciplines**. Through disciplined Word study, prayer and continuous meditation on the things of God and fellowship with other believers we will remain focussed on the Father. I learned so much from the life and disciplines of Frank Laubach. He trained himself to bring thoughts of the

Father into hourly segments of his day, no matter what he was doing. This is a discipline any and every person can do no matter what field of business you are in. If God is your priority, then He should be the priority in your mind and in **everything** you do. The slogan 'What Would Jesus Do' has to be taken literally until God's thoughts become our thoughts, this is especially important in the work place and home. The Kingdom lifestyle must be lived 24/7 or it is not a lifestyle.

From Fear to Faith

There is only one truly successful route to follow that can take a person from fear to faith and that is by surrendering to God moment-by-moment and day-by-day. Never forget who you are surrendering to. It is hard to surrender to someone who may not be trustworthy or in whom we have no faith or confidence. By giving the Father priority in our lives, we are giving our decision making processes into the hands of the Highest Power in the universe. It is He who will strengthen and encourage us to not give up and to continue in the battle. Faith is a battle and that is why we are told to put on the full armour of God daily. I love the terminology used in the Message Bible. Peterson captures the plight of all believers: *Ephesians 6:13-18 Be prepared. You're up against far more than you can handle on your own. Take all the help you can get, every weapon God has issued, so that when it's all over but the shouting, you'll still be on your feet. Truth, righteousness, peace, faith, and salvation are more than words.* **Learn how to apply them.** *You'll need them throughout your life. God's Word is an indispensable weapon. In the same way, prayer is essential in this ongoing warfare.* **Pray hard and long.** *Pray for your brothers and sisters. Keep your eyes open. Keep each other's spirits up so that no one falls be-*

hind or drops out.

For faith to work we must acknowledge that we are **unable to change circumstances on our own**. We cannot stop death, we cannot control nature's forces, we cannot change the hearts of people and we cannot move mountains, ONLY GOD CAN.

Mark 11:22-24 [NLT] **Have faith in God.** *I tell you the truth, you can say to this mountain, 'May you be lifted up and thrown into the sea,' and it will happen. But you must really believe it will happen and have no* **doubt in your heart.** *I tell you, you can pray for anything, and if you believe that you've received it, it will be yours.*

The focus of this scripture is the **heart**, not the head. **Faith cannot be reasoned in the head.** It is in the head, or the mind that fears are generated. We fear the things we see or cannot see, we fear the fact that we cannot change them, but in order to **not** lose control, we also fear giving it to God (makes no sense does it?). **Giving control to God means that we give up control**. Surrendering and acknowledging that we have no power or ability to resolve the situation. Surrender is to lay down our pride, humble ourselves and place our total being, our total decision making process in the hands of our Heavenly Father.

We must acknowledge and believe that a world without God is darkness and hopelessness. It is only His Word that can bring light to our souls. God wants us to have total, unconditional faith in Him in **every dimension** of our lives.

Taking Stock of Your Faith Level

I cannot go further without asking you these very vital question:

- Right now, **where are you** in terms of your faith level? Are you hot, cold or lukewarm?

- What is the condition of your heart in relation to **absolute** faith in God? Are you guided by your head or your heart when making decisions regarding situations that are pending?

- Do you have **more faith** in your **fears** or do you have more faith in God?

- How are you going to **raise your faith levels**, in other words what disciplines are you going to take that will grow your faith in the Lord?

- You need to sincerely pray and ask the Father to give you the spiritual INSIGHT into who He really is in your life. When you KNOW the Father, you will TRUST and SURRENDER to Him.

- Think up practical steps to bring Jesus into every hour of your day.

Week 3

Redemption and Deliverance
For Your Body

Week 3
Redemption and Deliverance For Your Body

One of the meanings of 'restore' is to **return from a ruined condition**. Well, that is exactly what the blood of Jesus did for us. He gave us a way to restore and redeem our broken, ruined, carnal bodies. Paul taught us that our bodies are temples for the Holy Spirit to dwell in *[1 Corinthians 6:19-20]*. When referring to the redemption of the body, it must be made clear that I am alluding to the sinful state of the carnal nature of our bodies. The physical flesh itself can be healed, but it cannot be saved, for we must all die once and then comes the judgement *[Hebrews 9:27]*.

Our bodies need redemption and deliverance on a daily basis. As I have said before, there is no quick fix. It is a daily walk, a daily surrender to the Spirit of God within us. For us to have any lasting success, we have to instil daily disciplines that will help us overcome the evil works and vices of the flesh. We often blame Satan for the things we do, when it is in our **power to choose** between right and wrong living. Satan provides the temptation, but we choose to yield or not.

We will also be touching on areas that actually need deliverance from demonic activities, where the devil has spiritually erected strongholds in the flesh and soul of a person. There is no reason to fear this, Praise God! We need to seek deliverance through the Word and the power of God and an even greater need to know how to **keep ourselves free**.

For those of you who are really having a battle with the flesh and struggling to break with old destructive habits, I would encourage you to do a water fast for a few days, or a partial water fast where you only eat in the evenings. Fasting will remove the obstacles that prayer alone cannot remove. Fasting is a very powerful spiritual tool. Satan hates it because it causes the flesh to submit to God and turn away from carnal lusts and appetites.

As you enter this final week of discovering how to overcome the flesh and transform your life, I want to encourage you to **maintain the disciplines** you have begun with during this time. The Father wants to be your constant companion, helping and guiding you through every day. However, He will only do so if you make the effort to include Him in all you do.

Praying, reading the Bible and doing what it says will totally transform your body, soul and spirit.

Day 15
My Body, God's Temple

---

*1 Corinthians 6:19-20 [CEV] You surely know that your body is a temple where the Holy Spirit lives. The Spirit is in you and is **a gift from God**. You are no longer your own. God paid a great price for you. So **use your body** to honour God.*

I am so grateful to the Lord that He did not say we must first clean our lives out and then He would come and live in us. The Lord knew that without His help this would be impossible. As a demonstration of **the power of His GRACE**, the Father came to live in our sick, sin-riddled bodies and helped us restore them to be fit vessels for His glory. Remember what I said about restoration, it is a **return from a ruined condition**. We cannot leave our bodies in a state of sin and not make an attempt to change. Change must become a permanent forward motion in our lives. **Ever moving and ever transforming.**

When this need for change **is not met**, believers do not make satisfactory progress in their Christian journey. Spiritual poverty and lack sets in like a disease, many times even taking on the form of physical sickness. I have often called this 'spiritual paralysis'. It's a fact of physics that no one at any moment in time is standing still. We are in a permanent state of motion because we are living on a revolving planet. When our forward motion is not towards the Kingdom of God we are moving towards Satan's domain and away from God's Kingdom. We call this process 'backsliding' because we are sliding further and further away from God's will and purpose for our lives. This ultimately leads to a life of spiritual mediocrity where a person is no good to themselves, no good to those around them and of no value to the Kingdom of God.

To fight the 'disease' of mediocrity we have to strive to walk in holiness. The real battle now moves from our minds to our bodies. *Romans 6*, deals with the reality that our bodies were slaves to sin and we allowed our flesh to dictate to and rule our lives. Christ now calls us to surrender our bodies to Him and make them slaves of righteousness. This process is called progressive holiness.

The dilemma that without exception arises for each of us, is how can we possibly gain control over the body that has had control for years? Paul clearly relates to this struggle in **Romans 7:18-20** *[NLT]* where he deals with his flesh and sinful nature. *I know that nothing good lives in me, that is, in my sinful nature. I want to do what is right, but I can't. I want to do what is good, but I don't. I don't want to do what is wrong, but I do it anyway. But if I do what I don't want to do, I am not really the one doing wrong; it is sin living in me that does it.* Paul in this agonising rendition paints a very vivid picture of the power of the flesh. It was only after much **discipline and spiritual maturing** that Paul gained the victory. In his epistles he shares about his victorious battle over the flesh.

Jesus Passed the Test for Us

The Father knew of our struggles and sent His Son Jesus to come in the FLESH to show us how we could **successfully overcome** the works of the flesh. In *Hebrews 2:17-18* it tells us that it was necessary for Jesus to be tempted **in all areas** just like us. Jesus was able to relate to our suffering and could therefore stand before the Father after His resurrection as our faithful High Priest and the sacrifice for our sin *[Hebrews 9:26]*. He never failed any test, therefore, through the power of His Holy Spirit He can now help us to overcome all our tests and trials.

We must fully comprehend that Jesus was NOT superhuman. He left His divine attributes in heaven. He was a man just like you and I, except without sin. He was raised a carpenter's son, worked for many years with His earthly father Joseph. Jesus learned obedience and submission to his parents and all the while His Heavenly Father was preparing Him for His short yet powerful three-year ministry. During His childhood Jesus learned to walk and talk with His Heavenly Father. Jesus with time came to know what His mission was. At twelve years of age He had already acquired great knowledge of the Word wherein was prophesied His coming and mission *[Luke 2:46]*.

Through the constant discipline of prayer and fellowship with the Father, Jesus learned to flow in the supernatural power of the Holy Spirit. He learned to hear the voice of the Father and He was obedient to follow every instruction. All this was done on an entirely human level so that you and I could learn from Him and imitate Him. Several times in the Word He instructed His disciples to do as He did and He even went on to say that greater works than these would they do *[John 14:12]*.

One Major Difference

There was one **major difference** between Jesus and all mankind, He never knew sin and contrary to us He never had to overcome the sinful nature. Jesus had to be the sinless, spotless 'Lamb of God' that would take away the sin of the World *[John 1:29]*. Jesus had to be tempted like us in all areas so that He could understand temptation and the negative power it brings to bear on our sinful flesh *[Hebrews 4:15]*. Jesus demonstrated to us how to overcome sin through the power of the indwelling Holy Spirit. His motive for coming was clear and plain to all who knew Him; He came to reconcile man back to the Father. He came to make us FRIENDS OF GOD. What a powerful statement and in *Romans 5:10-11 [NLT]* we read all about it: *For since our friendship with God was restored by the death of His Son while we were still His enemies, we will certainly be saved through the life of His Son. So now we can rejoice in our wonderful new relationship with God because our Lord Jesus Christ has made us* **friends of God***.*

He knew we were going to battle with issues of faith, forgiveness, holiness and other disciplines. He also knew that if we listened to Him and obeyed His instruction in the Bible we would have the same victory that He had.

Become a Slave of Righteousness

Romans 6:16-18 [NLT] Don't you realize that you **become the slave** *of whatever you choose to obey? You can be a slave to sin, which leads to death, or you can choose to obey God, which leads to righteous living. Thank God! Once you were slaves of sin, but now you wholeheartedly obey this teaching we have given you. Now you are free from your slavery to sin, and you have become slaves to righteous living.*

Our bodies will always remain enslaved, so rather choose to be 'enslaved' to the Father by **doing** His will. Enslavement is part of the weakness of the sinful nature. As we yield our members (body parts) to the Holy Spirit, we start the process of deliverance from the works of the flesh. Two of the most important verses in my personal life are found in *Romans 8:12-13*. We are not obliged to serve the flesh and its dictates which ultimately leads to death. Through the power of the Holy Spirit we must put to death the deeds of our sinful natures to live victoriously.

Choose to Serve God With Your Body

This is the reason why I suggested in the preparation for Week 3 that some of you may feel that a more intense fast is needed. Through years of walking with the Lord, I discovered that through the power of prayer coupled with fasting, I experienced wonderful breakthroughs in my life.

• Write down the struggles in your flesh and what you are trusting God to deliver you from.

• What measures will you take to ensure that you avoid the areas that cause you to sin?

To give a few examples:

Pornography, compulsive eating disorders, drug addictions, lying, stealing, bad temper, and you can add to this list.

Write down carnal struggles you are having and maybe you can speak to someone who is spiritually mature and ask them to help you by becoming your accountability partner. Seek counsel if you have an addiction that you cannot overcome. There is deliverance for all and you are no exception.

Day 16

Becoming Like a Child

*Matthew 18:3-4 [AMP] And said, Truly I say to you, unless you repent (change, turn about) and become like little children [trusting, lowly, loving, forgiving], you can **never enter** the Kingdom of Heaven [at all]. Whoever will humble himself therefore and become like this little child [trusting, lowly, loving, forgiving] is greatest in the Kingdom of Heaven.*

The Lord Jesus made a very strong and bold statement (above) when He was addressing the disciples on the issue of greatness. He was speaking on the condition for entry into the Kingdom of God. This reminded me of an incident a few years ago when my wife and I were attending a conference with Ken Blanchard as the speaker. What struck us and left an indelible memory was a statement he made regarding his salvation. He said something to this effect: "After 60 odd years I discovered the Lord and I have become like a little child in my faith". Here was this man, author of many books, a world-wide figure in the business world, but he sounded as excited as a seven year old who had received his first bicycle.

The subject that I would like to address is the comparison of a new believer to a little child and the fact that he must **remain in that condition** of childlike faith for the rest of his life. We know that children live in the dimension of the flesh and senses. They have yet to discover the world of the spirit, but their **hearts are wide open to receive spiritual input.** As a child I remember the amazing stories of David and Goliath, Samson and a lion he killed with his bare hands. These stories appealed to my childlike nature because they could be imagined and being a boy I was very drawn to the physical strength of these men.

Thinking back I realised that this is what makes a child special. Children have 'mountain-moving' faith. Unless they have suffered abuse and trauma, most children grasp at life as one big adventure because of their innocence. What do little children have that adults don't have? They are innocent, unaware of the power of sin and its ravaging effect on mankind. They find it difficult to lie and be deceptive. They are true to themselves and their hearts are pure and undefiled. It is only with time and maturity that sin sets in and fills the dark recesses of the soul and flesh. Paul had such understanding of this in **Romans 7:9** *[AMP] Once I was alive, but quite apart from and unconscious of the Law. But when the commandment came, sin lived again and I died (was sentenced by the Law to death).*

Paul states that there was a time that he was innocent and unconscious of the Law. However, there came a time of accountability as he matured from childhood into manhood and the law of God became alive and his conscience was awakened.

The Law of God is a direct reflection or mirror of who the Father is and what He expects of us. If man was able to live by the law, God would never have sent His Son. There was not a flawless man in all of creation that could fulfil His perfect law except His only Son. Jesus fulfilled the law and gave us a better covenant based on better promises along with the Holy Spirit to help us walk in God's perfect law of love.

Exposing the Dark Recesses of the Body

As we grow up and reach maturity, life shapes us and forms

us according to all that we are exposed to. One of the biggest attacks that Satan launches is against the flesh of man. Too soon those beautiful childhood experiences are lost and children at younger and younger ages are being exposed to the filth and rot of sick and diseased minds. The television or 'hell-o-vision' as I call it, has acclimatized the Body of Christ into accepting ungodly and immoral lifestyles, believing that all is admissible. You may have heard of the 'frog' experiment, but let me refresh your memory. Frogs were placed in a bowl of cold water. Gradually the temperature was raised and the frogs acclimatised to the temperature. Before long the frogs were boiled alive. Their acclimatised bodies did not detect the rising temperature. This is a picture of many believers in the Body of Christ being slowly but surely conditioned by the world and its sinful and enticing lifestyle.

One of the biggest enemies to date that has crept into our homes is the social networks, accessed through the Internet. We are living in an age where we cannot imagine life without the Internet. It offers access to amazing information and it has opened a world of knowledge and resources, but unfortunately the down side is very destructive. Statistics are horrific in Christian circles where marriages have been destroyed because of social networks that have replaced good old fashioned communication. There is such a hunger for relationships that young and old have found an outlet through the Internet. Facebook, Myspace and pornographic web sites are causing serious addictions and statistics of marriage breakups are bounding out of all control.

Don't get Dragged Back Into the Mud

Satan buries his hooks deep into the flesh of unsuspecting victims and without knowledge of God's Word and a living relationship with the Heavenly Father, many believers get dragged back into the 'mud' from where they have come from. In *Revelation 2:4-5* the church of Ephesus is warned against losing their first love. We as children of God have to continuously guard against temptations.

Jesus overcame all temptations so that we could walk in the same power and victory as He. When Jesus had His encounter with Satan in the wilderness after His forty day fast *[Matthew 4]*, He was in His weakest and most vulnerable state. The first temptation was against His flesh. You will agree with me that after forty days of fasting, food would be on top of the agenda. Esau couldn't handle one day without food and he sold his birthright for a pot of stew. On the other hand Joseph, when he was confronted by Potiphar's wife, tempting him to commit sexual sin, ran for his life. I want to address the young person who is doing this 21-day journey: Run from sin while you are still young and don't look back. Become as a little child filled with excitement and joy as you seek the Lord with all your heart.

Run for Your Life

We as believers are instructed in God's Word to run for our lives when confronted with sin that can take us out of the 'fight' of God's eternal plan. We are in a constant war zone against the works of the flesh.

2 Timothy 2:22 [NLT] **Run from anything** *that stimulates youthful lusts. Instead, pursue righteous living, faithfulness, love, and peace. Enjoy the companionship of those who call on the Lord with pure hearts.*

Don't be deceived and think that you can face a sinful situation and be strong enough to resist it. Paul would not have said run if it were possible to resist. We are not stronger than the devil in our own strength and the Lord will ONLY come to our aid **if we are obedient** to His Word. If the Lord says run, then He will protect us and get us through every situation.

Become like a little child, confess your sin and allow the Holy Spirit to dig deep into those dark hidden places of the sinful nature. I have often looked at children and wished that I was still living such a carefree life, untainted by the sin and evil that bombards us every day of our lives. Children have an incredible capacity to love and forgive. They never miss an opportunity to have fun and laughter is always hiding just below the surface. Repent and turn away from sin and enter the joy and freedom that is yours in the Holy Spirit. RESTORING YOUR FIRST LOVE should be the highest priority of your life.

Restoring a Childlike Character

2 Corinthians 7:1 [NLT] Because we have these promises, dear friends, let us cleanse ourselves from everything that can defile our body or spirit. And let us **work toward complete holiness because we fear God**.

- Seek after purity and holiness with all your heart. Establish the necessary disciplines that can help you overcome areas that are hooks in your flesh, dragging you away from God. Seek an accountability partner, a good and trustworthy friend, your wife or husband, your home-fellowship leader, your pastor or his wife and let them help you walk a road to freedom.

- Sin keeps us separated from God and in a state of permanent turmoil and stress. Restore your 'first love' with the Lord and He will guide you to still waters and a place of rest and peace.

Day 17

The Tongue,
An Uncontrollable Fire

James 3:3-9 [NLT] We can make a large horse go wherever we want by means of a small bit in its mouth. And a small rudder makes a huge ship turn wherever the pilot chooses to go, even though the winds are strong. In the same way, the tongue is a small thing that makes grand speeches. But a tiny spark can set a great forest on fire. And the tongue is a flame of fire. **It is a whole world of wickedness, corrupting your entire body.** *It can set your whole life on fire, for it is set on fire by hell itself. People can tame all kinds of animals, birds, reptiles, and fish, but* **no one can tame the tongue**. *It is restless and evil, full of deadly poison. Sometimes it praises our Lord and Father, and sometimes it curses those who have been made in the image of God.*

The tongue is the one member of the body that can defile the entire body. Like a fire it can burn out of control, killing and destroying everything in its path with the destructive force of its words. It destroys our bodies through negative confessions and has the power to speak death over situations instead of life. Most of the violence in the world around us is caused by the tongue. Fights and brawls are started because of the tongue. World wars have erupted because of foolish words spoken by boastful egotistical leaders lacking self-control and godly wisdom. Marriages have landed on the rocks because of thoughtless uncontrolled words and families are estranged because of unwise words spoken in anger.

James clearly states that the tongue is the one member of the body that is virtually impossible to control. Have you ever caught yourself speaking before you think? I have done so more times than I can count and it produced nothing but a harvest of thorns and thistles!

Words and Actions are Seed We Sow

Our words and deeds are seed we sow in the field of life. I think there is often more regret than pleasure as we reflect on past relationships and things we have said and done that caused or aided in the breakdown of relationships. You can repair a broken car and get insurance payout for goods stolen, but you can never wipe out the memory of words spoken in anger and frustration. My wife has often jokingly said that in many cases she has had to pray for 'crop failure' where actions and words have been used irresponsibly.

Verbally attacking someone is often a reflection of how little we value ourselves. When a person is strong and self assured, confident of who he is in Christ, he derives no joy from character assassination.

Make the Tongue an Instrument of Healing

Our total well-being hinges on our confessions. Life and death are in the **power** of the tongue *[Proverbs 18:21]*. I once read a book entitled 'What we say is what we get'. Job confessed that the thing that he greatly feared happened to him *[Job 3:25]*. When we confess fear we bring forth seeds of death and destruction into our circumstances but when we confess faith we speak Truth and Life into situations.

Proverbs 12:18 *[NKJV] But the tongue of the wise promotes health.*

What we confess over our lives, marriages, families, church

leaders, other people and our finances, affects us positively or negatively. We become enslaved by our words and beliefs. We can choose to be slaves of unrighteousness or slaves of righteousness, confessing, believing and walking in the Truth of God's Word.

Proverbs 15:4 [NLT] Gentle words are a tree of life; a deceitful tongue crushes the spirit.

The state of the tongue will reveal the **spiritual condition of the heart**. It is impossible to produce good fruit if the tree is evil. We can have righteous ideas and good intentions but the truth will be measured by what comes forth from the mouth. This is **especially true when we are under pressure**.

In *Matthew 12:33-37* tells us that a tree is known by its fruit. A good tree produces good fruit and a bad tree, bad fruit. Jesus was rebuking the religious leaders telling them that it was impossible for an evil heart to speak forth good things. Good things can only come forth from the treasury of a good heart and evil things from an evil heart. Jesus went on to say that on Judgement Day we will all give account of **every idle or careless word spoken**, in fact our words will either condemn us or acquit us.

Is it Possible to Heal the Tongue?

Humanly speaking, no, but with the help of the Holy Spirit, absolutely! This will require us to remain in constant, continuous fellowship with the Heavenly Father. By reading the Bible daily we will be able to renew our minds and conform our lives to the mind and image of Jesus Christ our Lord.

I want to suggest three steps to do daily that will help you to develop a godly tongue:

1. **Confess** your sins daily, **forgive** everyone who has sinned

against you.

1 John 1:7-10 [NLT] But if we are living in the light, as God is in the light, then we have fellowship with each other, and the blood of Jesus, His Son, cleanses us from all sin. If we claim we have no sin, we are only fooling ourselves and not living in the truth. But if we confess our sins to Him, He is faithful and just to forgive us our sins and to cleanse us from all wickedness. If we claim we have not sinned, we are calling God a liar and showing that His word has no place in our hearts.

2. **Pray in the Spirit** daily and you will stay in the spirit and come into God's perfect will for your life. By doing this you keep yourself in constant awareness of the Lord. When you are in God's presence you do not feel the remotest urge to sin. Make this one of your highest goals, to remain and seek out God's presence no matter when or where.

*Romans 8:26-27 [NLT] And the Holy Spirit helps us in our weakness. For example, we don't know what God wants us to pray for. But the Holy Spirit prays for us with groanings that cannot be expressed in words. And the Father who knows all hearts knows what the Spirit is saying, for the Spirit pleads for us believers in **harmony with God's own will**.*

3. Through daily fellowship with the Father you will have the power to **rule over you own spirit and your tongue**. The Holy Spirit will give you the ability to rule and reign with Christ in life. Have you noticed that when people hang around together, they take on one another's habits and behaviour? It is no different with the Lord. If we fellowship with Him and remain continuously sensitive to His presence, we will start **acting** like Him, **speaking**

like Him and **thinking** like Him.

Proverbs 25:28 [NKJV] Whoever has **no rule over his own spirit** is like a city broken down, without walls.

Proverbs 21:23 [AMP] He who **guards his mouth** and his tongue keeps himself from troubles.

James 1:19-20 [NLT] Understand this, my dear brothers and sisters: You must all be **quick to listen, slow to speak,** and **slow to get angry**.

Start the Healing Process Today

Today's spiritual exercise will be to practice the three given points:

1. **Confess** your sins and **forgive** those that have offended and hurt you.

2. **Pray in the Spirit** and set up little reminders to do so during the day until it becomes a good habit.

3. **Fellowship with the Father all through the day**. When you are in meetings, send up a praise offering in your mind. In your car, speak to your Heavenly Father, He is ever-present. Seek opportunities to communicate with the Lord, He knows your heart better than anyone else and He will make those opportunities happen if your motives are pure and genuine.

Day 18

Revolution of the Flesh

Galatians 2:20-21 [NLT] **My old self has been crucified with Christ**. *It is no longer I who live, but Christ lives in me. So I live in this earthly body by trusting in the Son of God, who loved me and gave Himself for me. I do not treat the grace of God as meaningless.*

The ONLY way to crucify the flesh is through surrender, for example: Making a conscious decision to give God the first thoughts of every day. This will keep you constantly aware of God's presence in your life. We cannot treat our flesh gently, there has to be harsh, disciplined actions taken. Remember the **flesh has a mind of its own** and will always seek its own will; that is why we so desperately need the Holy Spirit *[Romans 8:5]*. We have been enslaved to the flesh and its dictates for so long that extreme measures have to be taken to overcome. But don't despair, Jesus made it possible by going to the cross for us.

To help you understand the flesh and know what disciplines to apply I would like to quote from Dallas Willard in his book 'Revolution of Character'. He makes a profound statement about the body. He states: "The shoulders, the stomach, the genitals, the fists, and the face are constantly **moving us away from God** if they have not been **permeated by the real presence of Christ**". By analysing these bodily members, it gives us insight into the contact points that Satan uses to lure us away from the presence of God into his web of sin and deceit. Through this understanding comes revelation of how to overcome and discipline areas of sin in our lives.

The shoulders speak of us turning back to pursue sin, be it in gossip, or whatever has gripped our attention. I have often heard people say 'I just went back once, that was all'. Well, in most cases once was one too many and the consequences were grave. The Father wants us to set our sights on **Him** for then we will not want to look back. We will be too occupied with what He wants and not with what we want. We have to discipline ourselves to become CONSUMED with the things of God if we are going to have any victory over the flesh.

The stomach is a great stumbling block especially in the Western cultures of fast food and on-the-run lifestyles. People have neglected their bodies and the effects are disastrous for both them and their families. Obesity is one of the greatest killers in most first world nations. We must incorporate healthy disciplined exercise and a controlled eating plan. This must become a family commitment so that our children can also learn from our example which will set them up for life.

Sexual sin not only hurts those involved, but everyone around them too and most of all their relationship with the Lord. The biggest area of sin in young people's lives is in the sexual arena. This sin, if not dealt a deathblow, will follow through for the rest of a person's life, affecting marriages and forming addictions. These addictions affect the way one thinks and operates in life.

The fist represents words that evoke anger and fighting. The only person we must ball our fist at is the devil. Many people come to me to be delivered from a spirit of aggression or anger, when in actual fact they have a problem with the flesh. The flesh is not a demonic spirit from which you can be delivered. You have to discipline yourself to walk in love and self-control daily. Overcoming the works of the flesh takes daily disciplined action. You must take **conscious steps** to overcome the things in your life that cause you to stumble. Ask the Holy Spirit to help you and give you the power to overcome. Study the fruit of the Holy Spirit in *Galatians 5* and make a firm decision to incorporate the fruit into your life. The Holy Spirit must be your constant companion and if you remain in a state of repentance and humility, you will become aware of His presence. Slowly but surely, you will begin to discern His voice on the inside of you, guiding and steering you in the right direction.

The face (I need to include the whole appearance of a person), has become one of the biggest idols in our modern-day society. More money and precious time is spent on enhancing looks and appearances than any other industry. Deep rooted insecurities caused by worldly social pressures and a breakdown in the family social structures, have people seeking acceptance in the physical dimension. Social acceptance is often measured by what you look like, what you wear and what accessories you have and not by who you are deep down on the inside. External beauty which is but for a season, is far more pampered than seeking and desiring to strengthen and beautify the spirit of a person which is looked upon by our Father. Our spiritual growth should be the actual barometer for measuring actual beauty and maturity.

Satisfaction and fulfilment do not come from good looks, but from a good relationship with the Father and fellowship with other believers. Many are dissatisfied with their bodies and are forever seeking ways and means of 'improving' God's creation. So much money and energy gets spent on the flesh and so little on spiritual activities. Many believers would be spiritual giants if the time they used on enhancing their physical appearance were put into spiritual exercises.

1 Peter 3:3-5 [NLT] Don't be concerned about the outward beauty of fancy hairstyles, expensive jewellery, or beautiful clothes. You should clothe yourselves instead with the beauty that comes from within, the unfading beauty of a gentle and quiet spirit, which is so precious to God.

The Purpose of Disciplines

Children have been created to thrive on discipline and as previously dealt with, we need to become as little children again. When we were children we had to obey the disciplines of our parents. Discipline creates a secure and stable environment where boundaries are established to ensure safety and protection from personal, emotional and external harm. Nobody likes discipline because it cuts in against the rebellious and unruly nature of the flesh that always wants to go against the laws of God and perform lawless and sinful acts. For this very reason we need to harness the flesh and often times forcefully steer it in a direction it does not want to go.

1 Corinthians 9:27 [NLT] I discipline my body like an athlete, **training it to do what it should.** *Otherwise, I fear that after preaching to others I myself might be disqualified.*

Quoting from Dallas Willard in his book 'The Spirit of Disciplines', he states: "Disciplines are activities of mind and body **purposefully undertaken, to bring our personality and total being into effective co-operation with the divine order**. They enable us more and more to live in a power that is, strictly speaking, beyond us, deriving from the spiritual realm itself, as we 'yield ourselves to God, as those that are alive from the dead, and our members as instruments of righteousness unto God' as *Romans 6:13* puts it."

Here are a few disciplines that you can establish in your life to help you in areas that you are struggling with:

- **Prayer and Bible reading** should be a daily compulsory discipline. By doing this you guarantee success and victory in your daily life.

- **Continuous meditation** during the day causes one to focus on the Father and will enhance decision making processes, because you will be tuned into the Mind of Christ *[Joshua 1:8; 1 Corinthians 2:16]*.

- **Establish a prayer altar** in your home by reading the Word and praying together and you will find that this discipline will bring a new dimension of faith, unity and love between family members. It will build confidence and boldness in your children laying a foundation on which they can build their daily lives and futures on.

- **Take disciplinary steps** in your personal life over areas that you know are wrong and sinful. Pornography for example is rampant and it has crept into many believers' homes. You and your family need protection. Establish accountability measures to stop this destructive onslaught from destroying homes, breaking up marriages and brainwashing children.

- **Gossip and scandal is a destructive force.** If you are prone to this, create the necessary spiritual exercises to train yourself to stop. Spending more time with the Lord rather than with other people will break the vicious circle.

- **The discipline of avoiding wrong friendships** with the opposite sex, especially if you are married, is a very necessary precaution. Most times these situations create breeding grounds for intimacy where hearts are opened and the devil ultimately uses this to destroy marriages. My wife and I steer very far away from any such temptations. Remember, at first it is always innocent, but before long soul ties develop, emotions run high and the flesh takes over.

- **Create times of solitude** with the Lord. Jesus often went aside to be with the Father. It was in these times that He was refreshed and strengthened for the task ahead. We need to draw strength in order to cope with the stressful issues that surround us. Discipline yourself to make time for this.

Adopt additional disciplines in areas that you know are affecting your relationship with the Lord and ask the Holy Spirit to help and strengthen you to overcome them.

Discipline or Distraction

By not bringing in the necessary disciplines into your spiritual life you will continue on a road of spiritual distractions. Remember Satan is also a spiritual being and if you are not being led by the Spirit of God, you can be easily led and distracted by the spirit of the devil.

I mentioned the flesh and all the time, energy and money that are spent on pampering the body. I want to leave you with a challenge today. What time and energy are you going to spend with the Father, enriching your body, soul and spirit by disciplining them to focus on the Lord?

Discipline is a value that we cannot afford to neglect if we are going to walk in victory and success in life.

Day 19
To Lack a Little from God

*Psalm 8:4-6 [NLT] What are people that You should think about them, mere mortals that You should care for them? Yet You made them only **a little lower than God** and crowned them with glory and honour. You gave them charge of everything You made, putting all things under their authority.*

In every life there will always be the questions: Who am I? Where do I come from? Where am I going to? Without a deep rooted knowledge of our Creator, we will never know or find the answers. The Bible tells us that only a fool says in his heart "There is no God" *[Psalm 14:1]*. I found a very thought provoking quotation by Sir John Templeton in a book, co-authored by my dear friend, astronomer, Professor David Block, entitled 'Shrouds of the Night': "Would it not be strange if a Universe without purpose accidentally created humans who are so obsessed with purpose?" There are no accidents in God's design. Everything was created with purpose. When God blew the breath of life into man, He placed in us His DNA and the Word tells us that we have been made 'to **lack** a little from Him'.

This term I discovered in a Hebrew Interlinear Bible and then later in the notes of *Psalm 8* in the Dake's Bible. What confused me for some time was that some Bible versions quote this verse as "a little lower than the angels", while others again say "a little lower than God". I researched the meaning behind these two interpretations and Dake's shed interesting light on the subject. He explains that 'Elohim' being the Hebrew name of God was used in this context for angels who acted under direct delegated authority from the throne of God, in other words acted in God's stead. Thus we have been made 'a little lower than delegated angels', or 'lower than God' or 'to lack a little from God'.

Man has undoubtedly been wonderfully made yet on the other hand he has fallen desperately far from that original blueprint. Who could imagine that God could take a piece of clay, shape and form it into the image of Himself and then transform it into flesh, tissue, sinew, bone and all the parts that make up a body. The angels must have watched spellbound for this had never been done before. When the final moment of transformation arrived, the Father took this form that resembled Him, had all His physical attributes and characteristics and breathed into its nostrils the breath of His own life. His breath rushed into the blood stream, through the veins, got the heart pumping, activating the kidneys and liver and finally into the joints and marrow. Man became a living being. God had released His DNA into another being just like Him. What other creature did He call His children, His chosen generation and His special royal treasure? When Jesus, who was the first born from the dead, rose, He called us His brothers, sisters and friends and His Father once again became 'our Father which art in Heaven'.

The Measure of Man's Predicament

First came the fall in Eden, then a **'drifting away'** until man in his character and nature no longer resembled the Creator. To understand a measure of man's sinful predicament we need to start with the beginning of sin in the Garden of Eden. *Genesis 3:6 [NKJV] So when the woman saw* (lust of the flesh) *that the tree was good for food, that it was pleasant to the eyes* (lust of the eyes), *and a tree desirable to make one wise* (pride of life) *[1 John 2:16].* Can you imagine the Father's great disappointment when His special creation turned against Him? You can ask the question, "But in what way did they turn against Him for God had given them everything that they needed"? They had total dominion, control and authority over all the earth and all the things in the sea and in the air. The only command that He gave them was that they were not to eat from the 'Tree of Knowledge of Good and Evil' for then they would surely die. That day in the Garden when Adam and Eve heeded the voice of Satan, they were lured away from the presence of God and spiritually stepped into a destiny of eternal hell and damnation. They received knowledge, but not the kind Satan promised, for they discovered the 'father of all lies and deceit' and received into their hearts that same spirit. Instantly their relationship with their Creator was severed.

To Transform We Must Conform

Revisit Day 3 and read *Roman 12:1-2* as it contains the key to understanding the power of 'conformism'. We have to break with the cycle of sin by renewing our minds and becoming conformed to God's Kingdom **way of thinking and doing**. We have to become 'God-pleasers' and not 'man-pleasers' conforming to the social dictates and behaviour of this world. We have to be brutally honest and transparent with ourselves or we will not receive into our hearts the **power to transform** our lives. The flesh requires **brutal treatment** and like the Apostle Paul said, it must be crucified daily. The very thought of sin and conforming to this world's lures must be killed at inception. If we harbour wrong thoughts, they immediately breed and multiply, before long we are yielding to the same old sin once again.

James 1:14-15 [AMP] *But every person is tempted when he is drawn away, enticed and **baited by his own evil desire*** *(lust, passions). Then the evil desire, when it has conceived, gives birth to sin, and sin, when it is fully matured, brings forth death.*

Matthew 26:41 *[NLT] Keep* **watch and pray**, *so that you will not* **give in to temptation**. *For the spirit is willing, but the body is weak!*

In these scriptures we firstly see the **power of sin** when it is not immediately rejected in the mind. Secondly, the only way out of temptation is through guarding our hearts by continuously praying.

The only pure and godly force in society is the born-again Spirit-filled child of God. When measured against the backdrop of the Word of God, we are God's 'preservation force', being the salt and light to a totally distorted and perverted society. Through salvation, Jesus placed us back on track spiritually and redeemed man's original status with the Father.

Deliverance From this Lower-Life

In *1 Timothy 2:14* the Bible tells us that Eve was deceived and stepped into a trap, but not Adam. By this we construe that Adam was fully conscious of Satan's trickery. Eve went against God's instruction to remain under her husband's protection and Adam went against the Lord when he moved out of God's covering and disobeyed the instruction of the Lord. This is why a woman must maintain the covering of her husband or father or pastor at all times. By the same notion men must maintain the covering of the Lord and also their spiritual leaders. A strong spiritual covering prevents a person from being led astray. In a marriage there should be mutual accountability where sin and deception can have no place. This is God's gift in a marriage that has placed

Christ at its centre. In marriages where Christ is not at the centre, there can be no unity and secret sin can easily creep in. The Spirit of God is the Spirit of unity and will take you to the 'higher-life' whereas the spirit of Satan and this world brings disunity and disharmony and will keep a person in the 'lower-life' dimension.

Adam and Eve were created with a clear conscience and a pure spirit. They were totally receptive to the Spirit of God and there was no wall of division between them and the Father. After they sinned, they lost the 'higher-life' and moved into the 'lower-life' zone *[Matthew 10:39]*. The restoration only came about after Jesus rose from the dead and sent the Holy Spirit to come and live in man again. When we received salvation, at that point something very strange and indescribable happened on the inside of us. We became painfully aware of right from wrong. This inner knowledge does not come without tremendous challenges and we have to guard our souls (minds) daily from wrong and negative input. We must cherish the inner witness of the Holy Spirit when He leads and guides us to the 'higher-life' in Christ. If you choose to ignore that inner witness in your heart you will remain a 'lower-life' Christian battling day in and day out to overcome the onslaughts of the enemy with a slim chance of victory.

'Conformism'

A conformist is someone who behaves or thinks in a socially acceptable or expected way (Encarta Dictionary).

If God the Father made us to 'lack a little from Him' how serious are you about transforming your life to start resembling Him in your daily walk and life?

Every one of us is in a situation where we are expected to behave in a manner that will not offend those around us. Now you and I know that this is absolutely impossible if we are going to live the Kingdom-of-God lifestyle.

We are reaching the end of our 21-day journey and have had to make daily decisions of change in certain areas of our lives. This is what transformation is all about. Many of us have lived compromising lifestyles that we know in our hearts are not pleasing to the Father. We have had to make decisions to either change or remain the same. If we have chosen not to change we will always live with a void in our hearts, knowing that we are not pleasing our Lord.

My friends, take the leap of faith with me and decide that the only 'conformism' you will enter into is that of conforming to God's Word and walking in His principles and priorities. The spiritual freedom, gratification and fulfilment you will experience is indescribable. Yes! There will be battles, trials and temptations, but with the Lord on our side. We have everything to gain and nothing to lose except that which we need to lose anyway.

Day 20
Submission and Surrender Brings Unity

---

*Ephesians 5:21-23 [NLT] And further, **submit to one another** out of reverence for Christ. For wives, this means submit to your husbands as to the Lord. For a husband is the head of his wife as Christ is the head of the church.*

This scripture highlights the significance and importance of godly submission and surrender in its entirety through the marriage covenant. Paul was placing a wonderfully powerful mystery in the hands of believers. He was encouraging believers by telling them that their earthly marriages must resemble that of the heavenly marriage of Christ and the church. Paul writes of this great mystery in *Ephesians 5:32 [NLT] This is a great mystery, but it is an illustration of the way **Christ and the church are one**.*

The MYSTERY OF UNITY lies in its **power of unlocking God's blessings and agreement**. In *Genesis 11:6 [NKJV] Indeed the **people are one** and they all have one language, and this is what they begin to do; **now nothing that they propose to do will be withheld from them.*** When the Father saw the unity in the building of the Tower of Babel He realised that the wicked unanimity they had was not for good but for evil. He caused confusion by sending different languages so that they could no longer understand one another, therefore they could not agree with one another and the power of their evil agreement was destroyed.

The Seed of Life and Light

In a godly marriage there is unity of faith and love, so when a husband and wife come together in physical intimacy, the husband plants the seed of their love and life is formed in her womb. This seed is the life and testimony of the union within the marriage. When the Father through the Holy Spirit impregnated the virgin Mary with the 'Seed' of Jesus, she not only received the **Life of the world**, but also the **Light of the world**. Jesus could not come from the seed of natural man; He had to come from the Heavenly Father. The seed of earthly man had in it the curse of sin and death handed down from Adam when he sinned in the Garden of Eden. God had to break that curse once and for all. The 'Seed' *[Genesis 3:15]* of the Heavenly Father broke the curse. God prepared a day when His 'Seed' would be birthed on the earth, breaking the chains of bondage and bringing light and revelation to the human race. This 'light' would penetrate the kingdom of darkness, expose the enemy and empower mankind to overcome Satan's rule in their lives. Jesus came and reinstated the Kingdom of God in the hearts of man once again. The light and life that Adam had lost, Jesus restored. It is only in and through His 'light' that we can receive the revelation of God as our Heavenly Father. That is why it is so important to pray every day the prayer of *Ephesians 1:18* *[NLT] I pray that your hearts will be **flooded with light** so that you can understand the confident hope He has given to those He called—His holy people who are His rich and glorious inheritance.*

Jesus' Mission On Earth

Jesus' mission on earth was two-fold: Firstly, He had to **demonstrate the power of absolute surrender and submission** to His Father through His life here on earth. These two fundamental actions are the keys to unlocking the **revelation** and **blessing** of God and His Kingdom in our lives. Secondly, Jesus came to **deliver mankind from bondage and destroy the works of the devil.** If Jesus had violated His relationship with the Father in any form, He would have failed in His mission and all would have been in vain. We do not always realise that Jesus was human just like us and He could have failed if He chose to disobey the Father by refusing to go to the cross. That dreadful agony He went through in the Garden of Gethsemane was an emotional, physical and spiritual battle of His will versus the will of His Father. Jesus did not want to go to the cross; in fact He even asked that the cup of testing could pass Him by *[Matthew 26:42]*. Even though Jesus cringed at the reality of the suffering, He knew that He had to pass the final test of surrender and submission so that mankind could be redeemed. His obedience to the will of the Father was motivated by the purest love this world has ever known.

In *John 14* Jesus addressed Philip and gave Him the powerful revelation of the unity that existed between Him and His Father. Jesus did not leave it there, He went on to promise that if we believed in Him and do what He did then we too could have this unity and authority. ***John 14:12-13*** brings out the blessings and promises that submission and surrender will yield: *I tell you the truth, anyone who believes in Me will do the same works I have done, and even greater works, because I am going to be with the Father.* ***You can ask for anything in My name, and I will do it***, *so that the Son can bring glory to the Father.*

As we draw closer to the Lord we move into absolute light and life. The light that emanates from the Word exposes all sin and sinful deeds, convicts us of sin and draws us to the Father. It is so vitally important to understand the absolute necessity of a **daily** intimate relationship with the Lord. Without this discipline we become receptive to the **voice of the world** instead of the **voice of the Word**.

Protected by Psalm 91

I remember many years ago walking into a home that we had rented, I saw a sticker on the door which read "This house is protected by *Psalm 91*". This is exactly what we need in order to secure God's 24/7 protection. In a world of constant danger and temptation we are in need of God's constant covering of protection. Our protection is guaranteed through a daily relationship with Him. We will never overcome the flesh in our own strength, which is why Jesus kept repeating in the book of John that He only does what He sees the Father doing. As long as He was **continuously living in the consciousness** of the presence of the Father, Jesus was protected. It was His **spiritual disciplines** that kept him from the evils of this world and in this He gave us the example to do the same.

Intimacy, fellowship and obedience leads to **spiritual impartation**. Prayer is the womb, the incubation place preserving and nurturing the vision and dream God has for our lives. Prayer brings us into **unity with the Father** which births revelation and visions. As long as we are yielding to the works and dictates of the flesh we cannot hear the voice of the Holy Spirit.

No Short Cut to Spiritual Maturity

The Message Bible addresses the aspect of maturity in a very forthright manner and I hope you will take it to heart as I have. *Matthew 5:48 In a word, what I'm saying is, **Grow***

up. You're kingdom subjects. *Now live like it. Live out your God-created identity. Live generously and graciously toward others, the way God lives toward you.*

Every child of God has to make progress and mature in their spiritual walk with the Lord. This is the problem with a very large percentage of Christians. They are not on a spiritual journey. Many believers are just content to remain stagnant and passive in their Christian faith, believing that all is well. Nominal Christianity (in name only) is the curse of the modern-day church and this is an abomination to the Lord. Choose to live committed and surrendered lives, fully yielded to the purposes and plans the Father has for you. I guarantee that you will not be able to contain the blessings God has in store for you.

Relinquish Your Rights

God expects of His Kingdom citizens to **relinquish their rights** and give Him the full rule and reign over ALL decision making processes. This sounds so radical and it is. For too long we have allowed Satan and the world to dictate its lifestyle to us. Our decisions have been based on the prompting of our surroundings and the pressures of society. It is therefore only fair and reasonable to **give God the opportunity** to take over and help us to finally make a success of our lives.

Satan has built fortresses and taken control of areas in many lives. The Father on the other hand has taken ownership of our spirits when we gave our lives to Him. It is now up to us to **surrender and allow** the Holy Spirit into those areas that Satan has occupied. It is possible to have the Lord living in us and also experience satanic activities in our lives. Without getting into a theological debate, we need to realise that our spirits at the re-birth were inhabited by the Holy Spirit. Satan still has power over our soul and flesh until we surrender our thought life and bodies to the Holy Spirit. **Where Jesus lives there is life, light and freedom.** By relinquishing our rights to Him we loose the chains of bondage and discover a life of immeasurable blessings and exciting spiritual exploits.

In your quiet time today open your heart and allow the Holy Spirit to break down those walls of resistance. Root out every evil stronghold that Satan has erected in your life through the years. Every hidden sin that remains is a stronghold and will always be a barrier between you and the Father. God cannot relate to sin for He lives in absolute holiness, for He is holy.

Day 21

Our Home - God's Tabernacle

Hebrews 9:23-24 [NKJV] Therefore it was necessary that the copies of the things in the heavens should be purified with these, but the heavenly things themselves with better sacrifices than these. For Christ has not entered the holy places made with hands, which are copies of the true, but into heaven itself, now to appear in the presence of God for us.

We are in an eternal **Blood Covenant** with the Lord. When we received the Lord, we were born again into a covenant with the living God who shed His blood for us. Jesus' blood was pure and untainted. When the Father received Jesus' blood on the heavenly mercy seat our **redemption was sealed**. Visualise the horrors and inhumanity of a slave market where human beings are bound and chained to poles waiting to be sold. Slave masters haggle over prices, selling men, woman and children like cattle on their way to the slaughter house. This picture depicts us as the slaves, Satan as the slave master with our Lord Jesus purchasing us at the highest price possible; His life blood freed us forever from Satan's bondage.

I started with the Tabernacle and its contents and I want to end with it. Its symbolism provides us with revelation that directs us step-by-step into the presence of the Father. Think of the Tabernacle in the Wilderness. It was a place of sacrifice and repentance. When God's conditions were met, He answered with fire. This fire is the life-light of revelation. Without God's light, there can be no revelation.

The Preparation Process

When we go to the Father daily we must realise that we are living in a world that is constantly bombarding us with temptations. We therefore need to prepare our hearts to communicate with the Lord. The Lord showed me the significant relevance of the Tabernacle in relation to our spirit, soul and body.

The courtyard represents the body and was the place of the altar of sacrifice and the brazen laver.

- **BRAZEN ALTAR OF SACRIFICE** – This points to the cross and the place of sacrifice. When we go to the Lord daily we start at the Altar of Sacrifice. Before Jesus went to the cross, He surrendered His will saying, 'not My will but Your will be done' *[Luke 22:42]*. This is the **place of sacrifice, surrender and submission** all rolled into one. When we surrender to the Kingdom of God we **break our ties** with the devil and his rule in our lives.

- **BRAZEN LAVER** – Our next stop on the way into the throne room of the Father, is the Brazen Laver. This was made from the mirrors that the women donated. God gave us His mirror: The Word, and in it, the Bible reflects our spiritual condition. All flaws and imperfections in our lives are exposed. The Word represents absolute Truth; therefore we need to be honest and transparent when assessing our lives allowing the **washing of the water of the Word to cleanse us**. We lay bare our hearts before the Lord and look into His Word which is the perfect law of liberty *[Exodus 30:17-20; Ephesians 5:25-26; James 1:23]*. In the Old Testament all reference to the heavens turning to brass signified drought and God's judgement *[Deuteronomy 28:23]*. When the Israelites looked into the brazen laver it symbolised judgment of self, therefore we too must judge ourselves or the Lord will do so. We may very well experience a season of spiritual drought in our lives until we have dealt with all unsurrendered areas.

The second step is into THE HOLY PLACE which represents the soul of man. In this area we find the Golden Lampstand together with the Table of Shewbread and the Golden Altar of Incense.

- **GOLDEN LAMPSTAND** [Revelations 1:12-20] – Upon entering the Holy Place the first thing one noticed was the light. This **light symbolised illumination**. In the book of Revelation we see Jesus standing in the midst of the seven Golden Lampstands bringing enlightenment, correction and direction to the seven churches. Jesus is the Heavenly Bridegroom standing in the midst of His church, the Bride, wooing her and calling her into submission and surrender. From this light we see the TABLE of SHEWBREAD.

- **THE TABLE OF SHEWBREAD** – Jesus said "I am the Bread of Life". His Body was broken for you and me and we partake of His body and become His body. We are not only expected to read and gain knowledge of the Word; Jesus expects us be doers the Word and allow Him to live His life through us. We become an **extension of His Body representing Him** on earth.

- **THE GOLDEN ALTAR OF INCENSE** - We started off in the outer court with the **sacrifice and death** of the flesh and we end in the presence of God with the **sacrifice of prayer and worship**. In *Revelation 8* we read that the Altar of Incense that used to be in the Holy Place in the Old Covenant is now **before** the Throne of God. From this we deduce that when the curtain was rent a new dispensation of grace was ushered in and the church was born. An angel now stands before this altar in Heaven and catches up the prayers of the saints *[Revelations 5:8]*. Only 'living stones' which are the born-again children of God, filled with Holy Spirit fire can move on beyond the veil into the very presence of the Father.

- **THE HOLY OF HOLIES** – Our prayers have taken us beyond the veil which is the flesh of Christ *[Hebrew 10:19]*, into the presence of the Father. This is the throne room, which I call the **'revelation zone'** where the Father imparts His glory and knowledge to hearts that are fully yielded and obedient to His calling. The focus, the ultimate goal of every believer should be to achieve **intimacy and fellowship** with our Heavenly Father.

Incorporating Praise and Worship

In the last days the Lord promised that the Tabernacle of David would be restored *[Acts 15:16]*. In the first Tabernacle in the Wilderness they just had the substance with no praise and worship. David brought in a whole new dimension with His powerful Psalms and musicians. This ushered in the dimension of praise and worship into the Tabernacle of God.

Every morning as I enter into God's presence I go to the **Altar of sacrifice where I surrender to the cross**. I then move to the Brazen Laver and examine my life through the reflection of God's Word. It is almost like taking a daily bath and going through the cleansing process *[James 1:23-25; Ephesians 5:26; Titus 3:5; John 15:3]*.

Having dealt with my flesh and sin in my life, I am now ready to consecrate my soul to Christ and I enter the Holy Place. This is the place where we deal with the **mind**. E. Stanley Jones speaks of a spiritual heart attack, in other words, a dramatic **change of heart** and it also involves a **change of mind**. We have to renew our minds and the Holy Place is the place in which to do it. One of the daily functions of the priests was to trim the wicks and clean them of all soot *[Exodus 30:7]*. This is man's responsibility to 'unclog' all hindrances that will prevent us receiving **illumination and enlightenment**. It is here that the discipline of prayer is so necessary for it prepares us to enter into the presence of God. The soul will always resist God's cleansing disciplines. I have yet to meet a little boy who loves to bath. We have to crucify all soulish tendencies and distractions. The Shewbread speaks of the discipline of the reading of God's Word. Jesus is the Bread of Life and we renew our minds by the Word which is able to save our souls. God's Word is the constitution of the Kingdom and it contains everything pertaining to life and godliness.

Finally I am ready to enter the Most Holy Place and sit at the Feet of our Heavenly Father. This is the revelation and impartation zone. Through communion with the Father, He imparts wisdom, healing, life, purpose - the list is endless.

Preparing Your Earthly Tabernacle

This whole 21-day exercise was to prepare you to enter God's 'revelation zone', transformed and ready to receive what God wants to impart to you. Life becomes so uncomplicated and straightforward when we yield to the Spirit of God.

If you follow these simple steps over a period of time, it becomes a good habit and one that will reap a very rich harvest in your life. Wealth, in God's book, is measured by spiritual well-being. When our hearts and spirits are tuned into the Holy Spirit, we experience:

- The peace of God
- The Mind of Christ
- Daily wisdom by which to live
- The ability to overcome obstacles
- Light and illumination to 'see' spiritual truths

This is wealth beyond measure and is totally accessible to every child of God who persists in pursuing Godly disciplines. When we pursue godly disciplines we will not have time to get ourselves into trouble with fleshly carnal pursuits. A 'spiritually active' Christian will not desire to get involved with wrong and sinful habits that used to control and dominate his/her life.

About the Author

HAROLD, together with his wife Maud, has been in full-time ministry since 1987. After completing his degree in psychology and preparing to enter postgraduate studies, he had an encounter with the Lord Jesus Christ. This was to set him on a life-changing journey. He left the world of radio and television where he had been broadcasting for sixteen years and entered into the full-time ministry. On the 9th and 10th of October, 1983 he had two encounters with the Lord in which his prophetic office was confirmed seven times during the night by the Lord: Once on the first evening and six times on the second evening. This was a very sobering experience, but he never wavered and set out to prepare himself for the work at hand.

Today he is Senior Pastor of Little Falls Christian Centre and has seen the Church grow to several thousand members. With a tremendous team of full-time ministers, the local Church to date has planted over twenty Churches and almost as many Bible colleges, both locally and abroad. Harold is also the founder of Five-Fold Ministries International with approximately seventy five Churches and ministries affiliated to him. His vision and passion are to get the message of the Kingdom of God spread as far abroad as possible, while raising and inspiring many leaders to follow this pursuit.